SIKHISM

ੴ ਸਤਿ ਨਾਮੁ ਕਰਤਾ ਪੁਰਖੁ ਨਿਰ

ਭਉ ਨਿਰਵੈਰੁ ਅਕਾਲ ਮੂਰਤਿ ਅਜੂਨੀ

ਸੈਭੰ ਗੁਰਪ੍ਰਸਾਦਿ ॥ ਜਪੁ ॥ ੧ ॥ ਆਦਿ ਸਚੁ ਜੁਗਾਦਿ

ਸਚੁ ਹੈ ਭੀ ਸਚੁ ਨਾਨਕ ਹੋਸੀ ਭੀ ਸਚੁ ॥੧॥ ਸੋਚੈ ਸੋ

ਚਿ ਨ ਹੋਵਈ ਜੇ ਸੋਚੀ ਲਖ ਵਾਰ ਚੁਪੈ ਚੁਪ ਨ ਹੋਵਈ

ਜੇ ਲਾਇ ਰਹਾ ਲਿਵਤਾਰ ਭੁਖਿਆ ਭੁਖ ਨ ਉਤਰੀ

ਬੰਨਾ ਪੁਰੀਆ ਭਾਰ ਸਹਸ ਸਿਆਣਪਾ ਲਖ ਹੋਹਿ ਤ

ਇਕ ਨ ਚਲੈ ਨਾਲਿ ਕਿਵ ਸਚਿਆਰਾ ਹੋਈਐ ਕਿ

ਵ ਕੂੜੈ ਤੁਟੈ ਪਾਲਿ ਹੁਕਮਿ ਰਜਾਈ ਚਲਣਾ

ਨਾਨਕ ਲਿਖਿਆ ਨਾਲਿ ॥੧॥ ਹੁਕਮੀ ਹੋਵ

ਨਿ ਆਕਾਰ ਹੁਕਮੁ ਨ ਕਹਿਆ ਜਾਈ

ਹੁਕਮੀ ਹੋਵਨਿ ਜੀਅ

RELIGIONS OF THE WORLD

Series Editor: Ninian Smart
Associate Editor: Richard D. Hecht

SIKHISM

Gurinder Singh Mann

University of California, Santa Barbara

Prentice Hall Inc., Upper Saddle River, NJ 07458

TO THE MEMORY OF NINIAN SMART

A Division of Pearson Education
Upper Saddle River, New Jersey 07458

Copyright © 2004 Laurence King Publishing Ltd

10 9 8 7 6 5 4 3 2 1

ISBN 0-13-040977-4

This book was designed and produced by
LAURENCE KING PUBLISHING LTD, London
www.laurenceking.co.uk

Senior Editor: Samantha Gray
Commissioning Editor: Melanie White
Design: Karen Stafford
Copy Editor: Jacky Jackson
Picture Research: Julia Ruxton
Maps: Advanced Illustration
Printed in Hong Kong

Reviewers Louis E. Senech, University of
Northern Iowa, Pashaura Singh, University
of Michigan

Picture Credits

*The credits appear along with the pictures in the book. All those
marked with an asterisk * come from the collection of Rita and
Gurinder Singh Mann.*

Contents

Foreword 6
Preface 8
Note on transliteration 9
Timeline 11

Introduction 13

1: The Sikhs 14

The basic beliefs 15
The Punjab 17
Guru Nanak 18
Guru Nanak in Kartarpur 22

2: The Consolidation 29

The Sikh community expands 29
Challenges emerge 34
Guru Gobind Singh 38
Establishing the Khalsa Raj 45
Nationalistic aspirations 51

3: Modern Times 55

The arrival of the British 55
The beginning of the modern era 58
    Doctrinal debates 60
    Sikh conduct 61
    The Gurdwaras 64
The dream of sovereignty 66
Toward a world community 71

4: Beliefs and Devotional Life 72

Sources 72
    The Guru Granth 72
    The interpretive literature 75
    Court poetry 75
    The Rahitnamas 77
Beliefs 78
    Vahiguru 79
    Jagat 80
    Manas 81
Devotional activity 83
    Worship 84
    Ceremonies 85
    Festivals 86
Sacred space 87
    Gurdwara 87
    The Darbar Sahib 88
    Land of the Punjab 91

5: Society 93

Structure of Sikh society 93
    Vertical (social) divisions 94
    Horizontal (religious) divisions 99
    Personal authority 101
Women in Sikh society 102
At the turn of the twenty-first century 106
Sikh art 108

Glossary 118
Suggested Further Reading 123
Index 126

Foreword

Religions of the World

The informed citizen or student needs a good overall knowledge of our small but complicated world. Fifty years ago you might have neglected religions. Now, however, we are shrewder and can see that religions and ideologies not only form civilizations but directly influence international events. These brief books provide succinct, balanced, and informative guides to the major faiths and one volume also introduces the changing religious scene as we enter the new millennium.

Today we want not only to be informed, but to be stimulated by the life and beliefs of the diverse and often complex religions of today's world. These insightful and accessible introductions allow you to explore the riches of each tradition—to understand its history, its beliefs and practices, and also to grasp its influence upon the modern world. The books have been written by a team of excellent and, on the whole, younger scholars, who represent a new generation of writers in the field of religious studies. While aware of the political and historical influences of religion, these authors aim to present the religion's spiritual side in a fresh and interesting way. So, whether you are interested simply in descriptive knowledge of a faith, or in exploring its spiritual message, you will find these introductions invaluable.

The emphasis in these books is on the modern period, because every religious tradition has transformed itself in the face of the traumatic experiences of the last two hundred years or more. Colonialism, industrialization, nationalism, revivals of religion, new religions, world wars, revolutions, and social transformations have not left faith unaffected and have drawn on religious and anti-religious forces to reshape our world. Modern technology in the last twenty-five years—from the Boeing 747 to the world wide web—has made our globe seem a much smaller place. Even the Moon's magic has been captured by technology.

We meet in these books people of the modern period as a sample of the many changes over the last few centuries. At the same time, each book provides a valuable insight into the different dimensions of the religion: its teachings, narratives, organizations, rituals, and experiences. In touching on these features, each volume gives a rounded view of the tradition, enabling you to understand what it means to belong to a particular faith. As the Native American proverb has it: "Never judge a person without walking a mile in his moccasins."

To assist you further in your exploration, a number of useful reference aids are included. Each book contains a chronology, maps, glossary, pronunciation or transliteration guide, list of festivals, reading list, and index, while a selection of images provide examples of religious art, symbols, and contemporary practices.

I hope you will find these introductions enjoyable and illuminating. Brevity is supposed to be the soul of wit: it can also turn out to be what we need in the first instance in introducing cultural and spiritual themes.

Ninian Smart
Santa Barbara, 1998

Preface

Over the past fifteen years, a large number of undergraduate students who took my courses on Sikhism contributed to the evolution of ideas that appear in this book. These thoughts also served as subject for discussions with a whole generation of researchers, of whom Paul Arney, Anna Bigelow, Will Glover, Edward Maldonado, Dan Michon, Farina Mir, Anne Murphy, Kristina Myrvold, Caroline Sawyer, Gibb Schreffler, Ami Shah, Gurdit Singh, and Varun Soni deserve special mention. They have taught me more about the Sikhs and the Punjab than they could have imagined. My heartfelt thanks go to them all.

My gratitude goes to Ainslie T. Embree, J.S. Grewal, John S. Hawley, Mark Juergensmeyer, and W.H. McLeod for their continued support. J.S. Grewal and W.H. McLeod read an earlier version of this text and helped me refine the details of the narrative. I am indebted to Richard Hecht for his insights, Shinder Thandi for his critique, and the anonymous reviewers for their detailed comments. My thanks to Mohan Singh for creating the maps, Chris Gregory for giving them a finished form, Melanie White for her sympathetic overseeing of the project, and Samantha Gray for her helpful editorial assistance.

My warm thanks go to my family, Rita, Mana, and Raj, for their love and unstinting support. Ninian Smart, who invited me to write this book, did not live to see the finished product, but his mystic presence continues to soar above the place where it was written. It is an honor to dedicate this book to his memory.

Gurinder Singh Mann
June 22, 2003

Note on transliteration

No diacritical marks are used in the text, but the pronunciation of the Punjabi words is recorded in parentheses in the glossary. The Punjabi vowels /a/ /i/ /u/ /e/ and /o/ are fairly close to the sounds that appear in the English words *but*, *bit*, *book*, *bet*, and *boat*. A macron (⁻) s used to indicate an increase in the length of /a/ /i/ and /u/, and these sounds correspond to vowel sounds in the English words *balm*, *beat*, *boot*.

The Punjabi stops /kh/ and /ph/ correspond closely to the aspirated /k/ and /p/ as used in initial syllabic position in words such as *cat* and *pat*. The other Punjabi stops /ch/ and /sh/ correspond to English affricates used in words like *chair* and *share*. I have used /chh/ to indicate the aspirated /ch/ in Punjabi. The Punjabi /th/ comes close to the dental fricative used in the English words *thick* and *myth*. The Punjabi retroflexes /t/ /th/ /ə/ /əh/ /„n/, and the flap /„r/, for which there are no corresponding sounds in English, are marked with a subscript dot throughout the glossary.

Timeline

1469 The birth of Guru Nanak, the founder of the Sikh tradition

1520s The establishment of Kartarpur, the first Sikh community

1580s The building of the Darbar Sahib, Amritsar, by Guru Arjan

1606 Guru Arjan's execution by the orders of Emperor Jahangir

1675 Guru Tegh Bahadur's execution by the orders of Emperor Aurangzeb

1699 Guru Gobind Singh's renaming of the Sikh community as the Khalsa

1708 The death of Guru Gobind Singh and the movement of Sikh scripture, the Guru Granth, to the center of authority within the community

1710 The capture of Sirhind by the Sikhs under the leadership of Banda Singh

1765 The capture of Lahore by the Sikhs

1799 Ranjit Singh takes over Lahore and establishes the Khalsa Raj

1849 The annexation of the Khalsa Raj by the British

1860s Sikhs begin to migrate outside the Indian subcontinent

1865 The publication of the first printed edition of the Guru Granth

1873 The registration of the first Singh Sabha to meet the needs of modernity

1892 The Establishment of the Khalsa College, Amritsar

1920 The establishment of the Shiromani Gurdwara Prabandhak Committee

1925 The Punjab Gurdwara Act legalized the authority of the SGPC

1947 The partition of the Punjab at the time of independence of India

1966 The creation of the Punjabi Suba

1973 The passing of Anandpur Sahib Resolution

1984 Indian army attacks the Darbar Sahib and other gurdwaras in the Punjab

1994 The Amritsar Declaration demanding a separate Sikh state 1992

1999 The Global Sikh community celebrates the third centennial of the Khalsa

Introduction

In the spring of 1999, I received a phone call from the office of Governor Christine Todd Whitman of New Jersey. The caller had located my name from Columbia University's internet site and wanted me to help him obtain "biographical information about Khalsa." The Governor had been invited to participate in the "tricentennial celebration of the birth of Khalsa," by the **gurdwara** (**Sikh** temple) in Bridgewater, and it had been assumed that "Khalsa" was the name of an individual. The invitation, however, was to celebrate a major Sikh religio-historical event that took place three centuries ago and involved the elevation of the Sikh community to be the "**Khalsa**," a word originally from Arabic, meaning "the pure," and here meaning "the community of the pure."

Since there are only around 250,000 Sikhs in the United States, a lack of knowledge about the Sikh tradition is understandable. Yet this situation was indicative of the winds of change that are creating new realities. On the one hand, a small Sikh congregation such as that of Bridgewater is sufficiently at home in New Jersey to invite the Governor to participate in its religious celebration, on the other, the local leaders are open to accepting an invitation from a minuscule religio-ethnic group. A century-long movement of various religious communities from their lands of origin to the Western world is finally reaching a stage when the new arrivals as well as the host societies are becoming increasingly sensitive to a need to reach out toward each other.

<table>
<tr><td>The Sikhs</td><td>1</td></tr>
</table>

The Sikhs — 1

The Sikh community, comprising 23 million adherents, represents the youngest and least well-known of the world's monotheistic traditions. A large majority of the Sikhs lives in the Punjab (17 million), a northwestern state of India, while others have migrated to different parts of the country (4 million) and abroad (2 million). The Sikhs con-

stitute the most confident and thriving Indian religious minority, and have contributed significantly in the areas of agriculture, military service, and business. The siege of the **Darbar Sahib** (the honorable court), Amritsar, Punjab, popularly known as the Golden Temple, the most sacred Sikh pilgrimage site, by the Indian army, and the activities of Sant Jarnail Singh Bhindranwale (1946–84), the leader of the Sikh struggle for a separate country of **Khalistan** (country of the Khalsa), were extensively covered in the West in 1984.

The Sikhs who have left the subcontinent have done very well. There are over 600 gurdwaras, Sikh temples, spread throughout the lands the Sikhs have adopted. Many among them have had a record of considerable personal achievement. For example, Sukhi Gill-Turner is presently the Mayor of Dunedin, New Zealand; Kartar Singh Thakral is a billionaire businessman in Singapore; T.S. Nandhara, a well-known public figure in Kenya; Piara Singh Khabra, now second-term member of the British Parliament from South London; Harb Dhaliwal, a British Columbian minister in the Canadian national government. Dalip Singh Saundh was elected to the United States Congress from 1957 to 1963 and holds the distinction of being the only South Asian to have made it to this august body. These individuals indicate the range of Sikh settlement and the high level of Sikh success that have been achieved in various walks of life. Given the small size of the community in the U.S., Sikh leadership was sufficiently respected to be able to arrange an audience with President George W. Bush on September 26, 2001, and discuss with him their post-September 11 concerns.

The basic beliefs

Sikh beliefs are centered on **Vahiguru** (the wonderful Sovereign, the most frequently used epithet for God), who is the creator and the sustainer of the world. In this status, Vahiguru is fundamentally different from the creation and is beyond gender and other human distinctions. Vahiguru brought the creation into being with a single command (*kavao*), and runs it with the twin principles of justice (*nian*) and grace (*nadar*). Human life stands at the top of the hierarchy of creation and provides a unique opportunity to attain liberation (*mukti*), which is to hold a place of honor in the divine court after death. The Sikhs work toward achieving the ultimate liberation by living a life of social commitment, which includes the core qualities of hard work and service to humanity, while keeping Vahiguru, the sole object of Sikh prayers, in constant rememberance. Congregational worship serves as the primary medium of Sikh devotion.

The nature of the relationship between Sikh beliefs and those of the Indic and the Abrahamic religious traditions has so far defied scholarly consensus, but the Sikhs prefer their religion to be described as a revelatory tradition. At the fountainhead of this revelation stand the ten **Gurus** (the preceptors), beginning with Guru Nanak (1469–1539) and ending with Guru Gobind Singh (1666–1708). Guru Nanak believed that he had a special relationship with Vahiguru, and his poetic compositions served as the medium of revelation. Five of his successors created compositions also using the authoritative signature of "Nanak." He was assigned the title of Mahala 1, or "the first body in which the divine voice resided," and his nine successors were named Mahala 2 to 10.

Sikh revelatory writings were collected and compiled during the lifetime of the Gurus. Through a set of successive manuscripts created during the 1530s, 1570s, 1604, and the 1680s, these compilations evolved in a collection called the **Adi Granth** (original book), which was later assigned the status of the Guru Granth, the Guru manifest in the book. In addition to the compositions created by six Gurus, Guru Granth contains carefully selected writings of over a dozen bards at the Sikh court and those of fifteen Hindu and **Sufi** saints. Close conformity to Sikh beliefs served as the criterion for inclusion.

Following Sikh understanding of scriptural text as "the abode of Vahiguru" (M5, GG, 1226, here M5 stands for the fifth Guru, GG for Guru Granth, Sikh scripture, and 1226 is the page number from the standard edition of 1,430 pages), Guru Gobind Singh, the tenth and the last Guru, is believed to have established the Guru Granth as the living Guru for the Sikhs. The text has since enjoyed the highest authority within the community and has served as the center of Sikh devotional and ceremonial life. Both Punjabi, the primary language of the Guru Granth, and Gurmukhi, the script of the Gurmukhs/Sikhs, in which the compositions are inscribed, are assigned a sacred status (see the title page).

The Sikhs also believe that the events in the lives of the Gurus were part of the revelation, and that subsequent historical developments continue to reflect the divine design. As a result, the Sikhs tend to interpret their history as a set of sacred memories with each Guru leaving an indelible mark on the annals of time. The supplication (*ardas*) recited at the close of Sikh congregational worship constitutes a record of the historical memories of the community from its founding to the present day. Through this prayer the Sikhs express gratitude to Vahiguru for guiding the community's destiny in the past, seek divine blessings in dealing with current problems, and reaffirm their vision of establishing a state in which the Sikhs shall rule.

In line with Sikh understanding, this book follows the historical approach. The first three chapters examine the important figures in Sikh history, the ideological and institutional developments that they set into motion, and the points of interaction between Sikhs and other religious groups of the Punjab. Chapter 4 looks at beliefs and practices that have shaped Sikh religious life. The concluding chapter focuses on the composition of Sikh society, questions of gender and status, and briefly explores the possible future of this global community as it enters the new millennium.

The Punjab

The divine design for the Sikhs unfolded in the Punjab, a region which, accordingly, they embrace as their home and sacred land. The Persian term *punj-ab* literally means "five-waters," hence the metaphor for Punjab as the "Land of Five Rivers." In present-day parlance, the five rivers in question are Satluj, Beas, Ravi, Chenab, and Jhelum. The central Punjab has a rich layer of soil that has been made extremely fertile by the changing course of rivers, their tributaries, and heavy rainfall. This area, covering around 140,000 square miles, is demarcated by three natural boundaries: the Himalayas in the north, the Indus river to the west, and the Rajputana desert in the south. Three passes on the western periphery of the Punjab—Khyber, Gomal, and Bolan—provided the only land routes into the Indian subcontinent, and as a result, this region has historically served as a geographical crossroads where the cultures of the Middle East, Central Asia, and India have interacted in a myriad of complex ways.

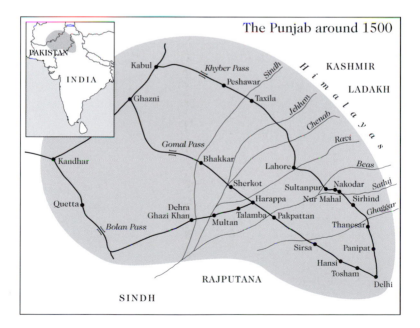

The Punjab around 1500

In the early phase of its history, the Punjab was a melting pot for people of numerous cultural and ethnic groups who settled in the region. These included the Aryans (fifteenth century B.C.E.), the Greeks (fourth century B.C.E.), the Shakas (first century B.C.E.), the Parthians (first century B.C.E.), the Kushans (late first century B.C.E.), and the Huns (fifth century C.E.). The first half of the second millennium brought the Afghans, the Arabs, the Iranians, and the Turks. By the fifteenth century, nomads such as the Gakhars, the Gujjars, the **Jats**, and the Kambos began farming in the region. In terms of religious beliefs, the Buddhists had disappeared from the Punjab, but the Jains, who were known for their atheistic beliefs and ascetic practices, had survived as a small community. The Hindu traditions included the followers of Shiva, Vishnu, and Devi (the goddess), and Hindu society was stratified according to a religiously sanctioned system of caste hierarchy. Muslim society was comprised of Sunnis, Shias, and Sufis. The nomads-turned-farmers believed in ancestor worship and reverence for local cults and tombs.

Guru Nanak

Guru Nanak's compositions and those of his successors serve as a primary source to understand his beliefs. From the bards at the Sikh court during the sixteenth century, Bhai Gurdas (1558–1637), a major interpreter of Sikh beliefs and practice, and the early seventeenth-century **Janam Sakhis'** stories about Guru Nanak's life, we find further information to understand the nature of his beliefs and map the important events of his life.

Nanak's parents were **Khatris**, a mercantile Punjabi Hindu caste, who in all likelihood were devotees of the Vishnu. His father, Kalu Bedi, was a patvari, or revenue official, based in a village named Talvandi. The patvaris were educated in Persian and the basics of book-keeping, and they enjoyed a high degree of authority in the social hierarchy of the village. The fact that Nanak's father owned land would have further enhanced the family's status. His mother, Tripta, came from a village named Chahal, located in the vicinity of Lahore, the cultural and political capital of the Punjab. Nanak had an elder sister named Nanaki, who later married Jairam.

*Nanak with Nanaki and Jairam. Gouache on paper, early
19th century. Courtesy of Punjab Archives, Chandigarh.*

In medieval India, as family professions were passed down through generations, it is safe to assume that Nanak's family would have prepared him for a job like his father's. This would have involved attending the temple-school to learn the basics of the Vaishnava/Hindu beliefs, learning Persian and some basic Arabic at the village mosque (M1, GG, 663), and training in account keeping as a member of a merchant caste.

In his late teens, Nanak married Sulakhani, who, as the prevailing norm dictated, came from a family of comparable socio-economic background. Her parents, Mula Chona and Chando Rani, were Khatris, and Mula was a patvari. He worked in Pakho ke Randhawe, a village in the fertile area of upper Bari Doab. The marriage was followed by a search for a job. In the early 1490s, Nanak arrived in Sultanpur, where his sister Nanaki and her husband, Jairam, lived. With appropriate presentation and contacts, Nanak obtained the position of storekeeper in Sultanpur, brought his wife along and spent a decade or so in this comfortable setting (see page 19). Nanak and Sulakhani's two sons, Srichand and Lakhmidas, were born here.

During the late fifteenth century, Sultanpur offered a rich and complex way of life to its inhabitants and this situation helps to explain the evolution of Nanak's world view during his stay there. The town was a leading center of Islamic learning, and as a result, Muslim scholars interested in religious matters regularly visited the town. As a provincial headquarter (*shiq*), many Muslim noble families, high-level revenue officials, administrators of justice, and interpreters of Islamic law lived and worked here. As a thriving center of commerce, the town also attracted a substantial trading community.

The location of Sultanpur on the highway between Lahore and Delhi enhanced its importance. A high number of political emissaries as well as Muslim pilgrims on their way to and from Mecca traveled through Sultanpur. The followers of Shiva and Devi on their way to ancient temples in Kashmir and in the Shivalik hills, as well as pilgrims to the Gangetic plains, passed through the town. All these travelers with their unique beliefs and practices would have added much diversity to the life of the townspeople.

Nanak's stay in Sultanpur came to a sudden end in the late 1490s. In one of his compositions, he briefly describes his visit to the divine court, his being in the divine presence, and the mission of spreading the divine glory in the world that was assigned to him

(M1, GG, 150). This powerful spiritual experience fundamentally changed the course of his life. He quit his position in the administration of Sultanpur to sing songs of divine glory. He sent his wife and children back to his parents' house and embarked upon a phase of extended travel accompanied only by Mardana, a Muslim friend from his village. Mardana came from the Mirasi background, who served as the village bards and recorders of family genealogies.

Nanak's extensive travels were spread over two decades and were distinct in nature. Unlike his fellow travelers, whose itinerary included visits to their own religious centers, Nanak seems to have gone to places of pilgrimage irrespective of their affiliations. This provided Nanak with the opportunity to observe life in its true colors. His compositions reveal a great degree of awareness of current political, religious, and social issues with comments on themes ranging from the Mughal invasion of the Punjab (M1, GG, 360, 417, 722) to the beliefs and attitudes of the various religious groups around him.

Nanak refers to Jains, Vaishnavas, Yogis, Sufis, and Ulemas in a way that reveals his intimate knowledge of their beliefs and practices. In one of his long compositions, for example, the **Nath Yogis**, a powerful ascetic group of the time, ask questions, and in the process of answering them, Nanak critiques their positions and presents his own (M1, GG, 939–46). In another composition, Nanak offers an early account of a ritual dance (*ras lila*) that is central to the religious life of the Vaishnava tradition in Mathura, north India (M1, GG, 465). His description of the performance of prayers (*arti*) raises the probability of his having seen the temple rituals at Jagannath Puri and Rameshvaram, Vaishnava centers in eastern and southern India, respectively (M1, GG, 13). There are also compositions that seem to have been addressed to Sufis and Muslim leaders of the time (M1, GG, 140, 721).

This phase of traveling ended in the early 1520s, when Nanak began to give his "mission" of spreading divine glory its final form. Having acquired a piece of land on the river Ravi, he founded Kartarpur (town of the Creator), and established a new community. Here, Nanak was revered with the title of "Guru" and his followers were called the Sikhs, which is a Punjabi term meaning "disciple." Since Guru Nanak's activity in Kartarpur constitutes his legacy to the history of the Sikh religion, this must be closely examined.

Guru Nanak in Kartarpur

Guru Nanak was a monotheist who insisted on the beauty and truth of this world. In his vision of life, there were no gender or caste distinctions and, through a life of ethical and social commitment, it was possible for both men and women to attain liberation (*mukti*), a place of honor in the divine court, the ultimate goal. Furthermore, he believed that a personal attainment of truth was insufficient in itself because individual liberation went hand in hand with helping others realize truth.

To understand Guru Nanak's actions during these years, it is important to look at Kartarpur, the town he founded. The immediate reason for the selection of the place seems to have been its proximity to the village of Guru Nanak's father-in-law. It is likely that he was helpful if not entirely instrumental in locating and then acquiring the land for the new town. Help from his father-in-law, however, could not have been the only reason for Guru Nanak's decision to found his center there. If comparison is made between the location of Kartarpur with that of Talvandi, for instance, Guru Nanak's home, several features of Kartarpur as a preferable site for the new community come into focus. First, the area is located on the bank of the river Ravi, which enters the plains at this point. The soil is extremely fertile—with heavy rainfall and plenty of subsoil water, it is excellent for agriculture, and thus provided an ideal location for building a self-sufficient community with a firm agrarian base.

It is also known that the area was in the process of development, as evidenced by the establishment of new villages during this period. As Kartarpur was quite central in this belt, it was well placed to attract devotees from the surrounding villages. The town was on the route to the ancient Shiva temple in Amarnath (Kashmir), and the Devi temples in the Shivalik hills. Consequently, a large number of pilgrims passed through the Kartarpur area. Thus Guru Nanak could meet these spiritual seekers and demonstrate the realization of his ideas in the life of his community, and, if convinced, they could join the new settlement. The location thus allowed the emergence of a core community and also provided for its potential growth in the future.

With the Himalayas in the background, the Kartarpur landscape enjoyed an idyllic setting and Guru Nanak's compositions show a great degree of sensitivity to it and the beauty of nature. Images of thundering clouds, flashes of lightning (M1, GG, 1273), lotuses, fishes, frogs (M1, GG, 968), herons, swans, cuckoos singing in mango groves (M1, GG, 157), larks cooing at dawn (M1, AG 1285) and dusk (M1, GG, 1283), and various meadows (M1, GG, 418, and 843) make frequent appearances in his writings. If the physical world was a divine abode (M1, GG, 580, 1257), then to him here was a beautiful fragment of that creation.

Kartarpur was also strategically secure from military or political interference, because it was located about fifty miles toward the hills, well away from the main Lahore–Delhi route, which invading armies coming from the west had historically taken. The site's potential to sustain a community with an independent economic base, prospects for growth, natural beauty, and relative security, were important aspects of Guru Nanak's vision for the future of his community.

What was the nature of the social and religious life that Guru Nanak created in Kartarpur? It is known from his compositions that he made no distinction of caste, creed, or gender for since there is a single creator, how could one hold beliefs in the distinctions between high and low, pure and impure, strong and weak, men and women (M1, GG, 83)? It is probable that Guru Nanak's family served as the core of the community, around which other families gathered. The doors of his community were open to all, although not everyone joined it. The limited evidence points to the likelihood that families that did join his community came from four backgrounds: the Muslims; the low-caste people from the Hindu social hierarchy; the Khatris; and lastly, the Jats and other rural groups who lived in the immediate vicinity of Kartarpur.

Very few Muslims seem to have joined the new community. The rulers during this period discouraged Muslims from leaving Islam and joining another religion; the individual would automatically lose the state's protection—not a prospect many people would have looked forward to. As for the low-caste section of Hindu society, their presence in the Sikh community is registered only toward the end of the sixteenth century.

As mentioned earlier, Guru Nanak himself was a Khatri, and it seems likely that relatives from his own village moved to Kartarpur. Relatives from his wife's side who lived in the vicinity of Kartarpur may have also joined their son-in-law's venture. Beyond his family fold, there would have been others impressed by his charismatic leadership and some would have developed links while continuing to live in their villages. Finally, the Jats and other ancillary rural groups, who were the main inhabitants of the Kartarpur area, joined Guru Nanak's following in large numbers. In all likelihood, they constituted the largest segment of the community at Kartarpur.

What was the nature of early Sikh religious life? With the family at the center of Guru Nanak's vision, life at Kartarpur seems to have been based on practical dictums. At the personal level, a Sikh was supposed to keep the body clean with a morning bath (*ishnan*) and the mind sanctified with prayer, which included among other things singing and listening to Guru Nanak's compositions praising the divine (*nam*). This was to be accomplished in the larger setting of a life centered on hard work (*kirat*), taking one's rightful share (*haq halal*), and contributing towards the collective good (*dan*). In simple terms, religious life was firmly framed in the values of personal purity, familial loyalty, productivity, and dignity.

Congregational prayer constituted the heart of Sikh devotional life (M1, GG, 17, 72, 1025, 1026, 1280) and Sikh men and women gathered and sang the praises of the Creator (**kirtan**), expressed in the compositions of Guru Nanak, accompanied by musical instruments. They offered thanks for receiving the gift of human life, and asked for a life of humility and service. The day at Kartarpur seems to have been structured around three daily prayers recited at sunrise, sunset, and just before going to sleep. It seems that while the first two prayers were congregational, the last one may have been recited individually or in a family setting. The singing of the prayers informed the devotees about the nature of the Creator and his relationship with the world. The Guru was at hand to explain these compositions (*katha*); after all, he was responsible for providing his followers with religious and ethical knowledge (M1, GG, 503 730, 938). At the closing of the prayer session, men, women, and children gathered and shared **langar** (a communal meal).

Work constituted the center of life at Kartarpur. There are reports of Guru Nanak helping with farming work. In an interesting episode, he is involved in weeding the rice crop, while Lehina (1504–54), later his successor, carried the wet grass for the feeding of the cattle. A portrait of Guru Nanak in an eighteenth-century manuscript depicts him conversing with a follower while another is running a Persian wheel, a system of irrigation, in the background. This was a model of respect for labor. While working hard, the Sikhs were to remember the Creator in whose hands was the final outcome of their endeavor. They had to sow and weed the crops; the harvest, however, was a divine gift.

Guru Nanak's model of ideal living in Kartarpur was different from those of his neighbors. As a believer in Vahiguru, Guru Nanak could not accept the Jain belief system, in which the divinity was simply absent, and he regarded their ascetic practices of pulling hair and not bathing as desecrations of the body (M1, GG, 150). He was also convinced that the Hindu search for liberation centered on image worship was futile (M1, GG, 637). The Nath Yogis' belief in solitary meditation and rejection of family life had no appeal to him. While the Yogis may have perceived their centers situated on high mounds and in caves as markers of spiritual elevation, standing above the villages of the plains, the Guru regarded their monastic way of life as a form of social escapism (M1, GG, 1245).

Although sharing a belief in an all-powerful Creator, Guru Nanak questioned the practices of Islamic orthodoxy. However, in the founding of the Kartarpur community, there is a pattern that parallels the lives of Sufi masters, many of whom traveled to distant centers (*khanqahs*) in the early stages of their lives and finally settled down to establish one of their own. At these centers, which were generally these Sufi saints' homes, they imparted religious learning to those who lived around them and provided shelter and food for travelers. Based on the belief that they should serve the common people and maintain cordial relationships with them, Sufi masters fed the hungry and tended to the sick who were living in the vicinity.

Expanding on this vision of giving service to fellow beings, Guru Nanak created a constituency that was far more comprehensive than that of a typical Sufi center. Although it contained families and fulfilled their material, moral, and religious needs, Guru Nanak's conception of his role was significantly different from that of many Sufi masters. He had no use for the extended meditation sessions, during which the Sufis abstained from food and drink and subjected themselves to ascetic practices. Nor was he open to making claims of power that could guarantee a higher level of spirituality for others, as some Sufis and Yogis did (M1, GG, 1286).

After establishing the community, Guru Nanak consciously worked toward providing it with distinct structures and an understanding of itself as a group. For Guru Nanak, he was the founder with his followers (M1, GG, 503), and leaders of all kinds whatever, religious, political, or military, enjoyed divine support (M1, GG, 145). He also saw himself as the medium of the divine message, and in this special status, he formulated beliefs for those who were willing to follow him. He worked in the fields to show respect for labor, and established models of behavior for his followers. He also debated religious and social matters with those who were interested.

It is important to point out that he was not simply a religious figure but the overall leader of the community. Writing in the 1540s, Satta and Balvand, two bards at the Sikh court, report the founding of Kartarpur in political terms embellishing it with royal metaphors such as the "creation of a castle," "the striking of a coin," and calling the ceremony of the Guru's succession the "royal coronation" (GG, 966–67). An entry in the Goindval Pothis, a manuscript compiled in the early 1570s, describes Guru Nanak as, "Emperor Bedi protective of matters religious and temporal." (See page 27.)

The fact that Guru Nanak elevated a successor to his position indicates the seriousness with which he regarded his office. His selection of a single successor during his own lifetime distinguishes the Sikh model of succession from those of the Sufis and Nath Yogis, who appointed multiple successors or who became successors by virtue of their being disciples. In the case of the Sufis, their children were normally the successors. For Guru Nanak, spiritual merit rather than a biological link was the sole criterion of selection.

Working within a context in which contemporary saints made use of the vernacular for their compositions, Guru Nanak wrote in Punjabi, but he made sure that his "new revelation" was recorded in a distinct script, **Gurmukhi**. He believed that those who sang his compositions recorded in the new script would attain liberation (M1, GG, 432). By this time, paper was available in the Punjab and Guru Nanak recorded his compositions in the form of a volume (*pothi*), a revelatory text and a precious possession of the community. From early accounts of the succession ceremony (*dastarbandhi*), we know that the placing of this volume in the hands of his successor marked the actual passing of the authority from the Guru.

Being a divine creation, the whole world is sacred for the Sikhs. However, the gurdwara, the house of the Guru, for example, enjoyed a special status within it. The Sikhs met there to pray, receive ethical and metaphysical knowledge, and share *langar* (M1, GG, 153, 730,

<table>
<tr><td>The Consolidation</td><td>2</td></tr>
</table>

This chapter briefly examines the developments during the three centuries after Guru Nanak's death in 1539 to the period of Ranjit Singh (1780–1839), the most powerful political figure to have emerged in Sikh history. The period is discussed under four headings: the early expansion of the Sikh community; the response of the Mughal administration to this development; Sikh revitalization under Guru Gobind Singh; and the establishment of the Khalsa Raj. In the process, we will trace the rise of the Sikhs as the third major religious and political community within Punjabi society.

The Sikh community expands

As mentioned above, Guru Nanak selected a successor whose early name was Lehina and elevated him to the position of Guru during his lifetime. We know that he was married, his wife's name was Khivi, and they belonged to a village named Khadur. The Janam Sakhis report that in one of his pilgrimages to a Devi temple in the hills Lehina visited Kartarpur and, after meeting Guru Nanak, his spiritual search came to an end, with the result that he, and in all likelihood his family, moved to Kartarpur.

While at Kartarpur, Lehina worked hard and received the recognition of his new Guru (Satta and Balvand, GG, 967). He may have been one of the best educated among the Sikhs since references tell that at Kartarpur he helped to order and inscribe the compositions of Guru Nanak in volume form. This work would have given him a close acquaintance, if not a mastery, of Guru Nanak's compositions and the themes expressed in them. In the sixty-two couplets he himself composed, he sings of the nature of divine command (M2, GG, 1239), the equality of all humans (M2, GG, 1238), and the importance of the Guru in one's search for liberation (M2, GG, 1237). In the late 1530s, Guru Nanak gave him a new name, Angad (my limb), elevated him to the office of the Guru, and thus, as far he was able, ensured a smooth transition of authority.

After Guru Nanak's death, however, his eldest son, Srichand (b. 1494), challenged Guru Angad's authority and claimed to be the rightful successor to his father's position. Guru Angad described Srichand's action as "self-elevation," and summarily rejected it. However, because Mughal law recognized sons as the rightful owners of their father's properties, Guru Angad decided to return to his native village, Khadur, and establish his seat of authority there. Sikh poets Satta and Balvand sing of Guru Angad's "throne with hundred branches," his "thriving court," and the numerous followers who came there to "remove their rust" and "feast at his spiritual *langar*." Mata Khivi, the Guru's wife, served delicacies of many types at the thriving temporal *langar* at Khadur (GG, 967).

The first succession set the model for those that followed. Here, Guru Nanak appointed a successor, who was believed to be in complete unison with the Guru, in the sense that a flame had immersed itself into another (Satta and Balvand, GG, 967). The founder's son, however, asserted his right to his father's property, and developed a competing seat of authority. The nominated successor, who received support from the majority of his predecessor's followers, in turn, was forced to move with his family to a new place, and build a community there, according to the model established at Kartarpur.

Three Gurus, Guru Amardas (1470–1574), Guru Ramdas (1534–1584), and Guru Arjan (1563–1606) provided leadership during the second half of the sixteenth century. After Guru Nanak, his successors continued to compose verses that highlighted the Guru as the medium of revelation. They elaborated on the themes available in the founder's writings and also sang of the unity of Guruship and the centrality of the Guru's role for those seeking liberation (M3, GG, 66, 86).

In these verses, the Sikh community emerges as a theme in its own right (M4, GG, 304, 305, 667, and 1116), being described as having a path that was sharper than the edge of a sword and thinner than the human hair (M3, GG, 918; M5, GG, 534), but it guaranteed a place in the divine court (M3, GG, 33) and was consequently felt to be superior to other beliefs available at that time (M3, GG, 360). To create

The Darbar Sahib. R.M. Singh. Oil on board, 2002. *

a conducive environment to help those families who were willing to join this difficult path, the Gurus built new towns: Guru Amardas established Goindval (city of Govind, an epithet for Vahiguru in early Sikh writings); Guru Ramdas founded Ramdaspur (town of Ramdas); and Guru Arjan expanded Ramdaspur and also founded three new towns—Tarn Taran, Sri Gobindpur (later named Sri Hargobindpur), and a new Kartarpur.

In the Sikh belief system, Ramdaspur was a divine town. The Darbar Sahib, a majestic structure built inside "a pool of nectar" (*amritsar*), constituted its public center. (See above.) The town was believed to have the protection of truth and justice, and its fortifications were established on the grounds of divine knowledge (M5, GG, 430). In short, according to Guru Arjan, there was no place like Ramdaspur on the face of this earth (M5, GG, 1362).

In these new towns, Sikh devotional life remained centered on congregational worship. Making a pilgrimage to Ramdaspur began to be considered a devout activity, since a bath in the pool there washed away the sins of the devotee (M5, GG, 623). The visit also included participation in the congregational prayers, an audience with the Guru, listening to his sermon, meeting fellow Sikhs and partaking of the *langar*. The prayers became more elaborate as the compositions of Gurus Amardas, Ramdas, and Arjan were added to the liturgical texts used at Kartarpur.

Sikh sacred literature expanded as each Guru added new compositions and thereby updated the sacred text. In the 1570s, the Sikhs compiled a four-volume text, which later came to be known as the Goindval Pothis. Guru Arjan added his own and his father's compositions to the contents of the Goindval Pothis and created what became known as the Kartarpur Pothi. These manuscripts attained increasing authority within the community. At the time of Guru Amardas's succession in 1574, his son Mohan made his claim for Guruship by virtue of physical possession of the Goindval Pothis. Later, a branch of Guru Arjan's descendents would present the Kartarpur Pothi as a symbol of their authority. The centrality of the manuscripts in these claims further added to their importance in the eyes of their custodians. Two of the Goindval Pothis and the entire Kartarpur Pothi are still in existence and, as proto-scriptural texts, they are a unique possession of the Sikh community.

Guru Nanak refers to **Rahit** (M1, GG, 831, 1343), which is the code of belief and conduct that the Sikhs were expected to follow. His successors elaborated on his ideas. According to Guru Ramdas, the code included waking early, bathing, reciting the Sikh sacred verses, joining the congregation and listening to the advice of the Guru, while keeping the divine constantly in your thoughts (M4, GG, 305). Bhai Gurdas sings of the importance of service along with prayer in Sikh life.

After his death, the Sikhs developed stories around the life of Guru Nanak. Some of those who had known him at Kartarpur would have been happy to narrate to newcomers, as well as to the younger generation of followers, their memories of the founder. Guru Nanak's extensive travels offered these storytellers fertile ground to establish the religious supremacy of the "master" of the tradition they followed. In the process, a rich Sikh mythology was created around Guru Nanak's life. These stories were written down, and some of these manuscripts were illustrated in considerable artistic detail.

The community continued to expand both in numbers and in the variety of social backgrounds of newcomers. By the end of the sixteenth century, there are references to people from a wide variety of Hindu castes, as well as from among the Muslims, becoming Sikhs. To maintain close contact with distant congregations, Guru Amardas introduced a system of authority called the **manji** (cot, in essence seat of authority). Initially, there were over twenty of these, spread across the central Punjab. The members of these congregations were encouraged to visit the center, and soon Vaisakhi (spring) and Divali (fall), two pre-existing harvest festivals, were appropriated as occasions for visits to Goindval and later to Ramdaspur.

It was Guru Ramdas who introduced the office of the **Masand** (a place of honor) to the holder of the authority at the *manjis*. Those so honored were the nominees of the Gurus and their duties included leading congregational prayers, providing doctrinal guidance to their constituents, bringing new people to the fold, as well as serving as links between the local congregations and the center.

During Guru Arjan's time, charity was institutionalized as a "tithe" (*dasvandh*), and all Sikh families had to contribute one tenth of their produce toward the central treasury (*Guru di golak*) to be used for the welfare of the community. The tithe strengthened the collective Sikh resources while simultaneously serving as an individual family's expression of gratitude for the divine bounty. The *langar* also worked as a medium for service and a marker of Sikh philanthropy since it was open for all to partake.

Sikh belief in social commitment and service expanded beyond their own community. The digging of wells and tanks was a typical act of philanthropy performed by religious and political figures of the time. Guru Amardas, for instance, established a large well with stairs (*bauli*) at Goindval to provide drinking water for the people living there. Guru Arjan had several wells and tanks dug in the area, including a well with stairs to provide water for the residents of Lahore. His compositions tell of the importance of helping others (*parupkar*, M5, GG, 533, 815), and sharing the divine gifts with all (*sanjhival*, M5, GG, 97). The Gurus also asked for the divine grace on all humanity (M3, GG, 853; M5, GG, 1251, 1357, 1358).

Sikh towns and the mapping of the *manjis* indicate that by the end of the sixteenth century the Sikhs were well entrenched in central Punjab. Bhai Gurdas refers to the Gurus' praise resounding in the Punjab as well as in towns such as Bukhara, Kabul, Lahore, Delhi, Agra, Banaras, and Patna, which were all situated on the trade route connecting central Asia with eastern India. There are also references to Sikhs living in coastal towns in the south and Kashmir in the north.

A strand of thinking centered on a belief in Sikh territorial autonomy began to emerge at this point. References to territorial boundaries appear in Guru Nanak's compositions; after all, both his father and his father-in-law measured people's fields in order to assess the revenue they owed (*rakhu*, M1, GG, 595). The Jats who joined the Sikh fold in large numbers have been known for their profound hostility to any infringement on their areas (*juh*). As referred to above, the Sikhs saw the founding of Kartarpur as the "creation of a castle," or a self-subsisting autonomous unit.

Guru Arjan described Ramdaspur as the center of Sikh territory (*des*, M5, GG, 807, 1141), and the capital of their kingdom of humility (M5, GG, 74, 816), which did not demand taxes (M5, GG, 430). When the Bhatts, a high-caste group, joined the Sikh court during this time as resident poets, they spoke of its throne, canopies, ceremonial flywhisks, flags, and the overall majesty of the Sikh center (GG, 1393, 1407). In their eyes, the Guru's position was an extension of the times of King Janak, a sage and a king in Hindu mythology, and for them, the Guru was the Sacha Patshah (true king), while the Mughals and others held false authority.

The self-definition of the Sikh community developed considerably, and by the start of the seventeenth century, it had a sacred text, a sacred mythology, a sacred geography, and a sacred calendar with a leader who decided their belief system and practice, and was emphatic that his path was distinct from those followed by Hindus and Muslims (M5, GG, 885, and 1136). The realization that the Sikhs constituted a distinct religious group was evident to outsiders as well. *Dabistan-i-Mazahib*, an important non-Sikh document of the period, assigns the Sikhs an autonomous status and actually places them not with the Hindu groups but alongside the Sufis.

Challenges emerge

The Mughal authorities were certainly aware of the presence of the evolving Sikh community in the mid-sixteenth century. Goindval was situated on the main route from Lahore to Delhi, while the Jats, who were the main constituent of the community, were the key source of revenue for the Mughal treasury. In fact, at the end of the century, official records report a meeting between Emperor Akbar (1556–1605) and Guru Arjan in 1598.

During Guru Amardas's time, the people living in the vicinity of Goindval are reported to have complained against him to the Lahore administration (M4, GG, 306), and later, Guru Arjan refers to a formal complaint (*mahazar*) lodged against him at Lahore (M5, GG, 199), which seemingly resulted in the Lahore administration's sending Sulahi Khan, a local official, to resolve the problem. On the way to Ramdaspur, however, Sulahi Khan died in an accident (M5, GG, 825) and the matter seems to have been shelved. Emperor Akbar's attitude of religious liberalism did not allow these tensions to attain serious form and the Sikh community continued to thrive.

After the death of Emperor Akbar, however, it is certain that the new emperor, Jahangir (r. 1605–1627), regarded Guru Arjan's position at Ramdaspur as problematic and felt the need to contain his authority. Jahangir disapproved of Guru Arjan's support for Khusrau, the rebel Mughal prince who passed through the Punjab, and also held in disdain the Guru's attracting "some ignorant and silly Muslims" to his fold. In his own words, he had two solutions: either to "put an end" to "this shop of falsehood," or to "bring it into the fold of Islam." He ordered Murtaza Khan, the governor of Lahore, "to confiscate Arjan's property and execute him." Guru Arjan was ordered to present himself at Lahore, where he was executed in 1606.

With Guru Arjan's succession, the office of the Guru had become hereditary, and Hargobind (1595–1644), his only son, succeeded him. At the ceremony, however, Sikh tradition shows him to have worn two swords, symbolizing his twin authority as the master of the spiritual (***din**/piri*) as well as the temporal (***duniya**/miri*) concerns of the community. If this did happen, it was simply a formal declaration of what had been part of Sikh thinking since the days of Guru Nanak, that is, that the Guru was the overall leader of the community.

The Darbar Sahib continued to serve as the venue for congregational prayers, and the main strands of Sikh religious life remained intact. In addition, Guru Hargobind had a platform constructed in its vicinity where he could formally conduct his temporal duties. This platform later developed into the ***Akal Takhat*** (throne of the Timeless One), the importance of which is discussed in Chapter 4 (see

p. 89). The Sikhs also erected Lohgarh (iron fort) for the defense of Ramdaspur. The Guru encouraged the Sikhs to bring weapons and horses as part of the tithe. Guru Arjan had declared the need for barbed bushes around the community's territory (M5, GG, 521), and Bhai Gurdas alludes to Guru Hargobind's practice of raising thorny trees on Sikh territorial boundaries.

However, the event of Guru Arjan's death brought into focus the Sikh emphasis on a life of honor and fearlessness. For Guru Nanak, life without dignity was not worth living (M1, GG, 142, 223, and 940), and Guru Amardas had echoed that opinion (M3, GG, 358, 555, and 842), while Guru Arjan had gone a step further to consider fearlessness as a divine gift to be equated with liberation itself (M5, GG, 498, 702, 809, 820, 1184, 1236 and 1299). Sikh ideology pointed in the direction of rejecting oppression of any kind—the Mughal authority in this case—and the social constituency of the Sikhs had the requisite strength to support this attitude. The Jats, who had a history of defiance against authority, would have had no compunction in resisting any onslaught on the community's autonomy. As it turned out, the Mughals did not take a firm stance this time and some sort of coexistence between the two was worked out.

With the death of Jahangir and ascent of Shah Jahan to the throne in Delhi (r. 1627–1658), the tensions resurfaced. Guru Hargobind's decision to leave Ramdaspur temporarily and visit the Malwa region did not help. On his return, the Lahore administration engaged the Sikhs in a series of battles, which resulted in the Guru's decision to move his center to the Shivalik hills, where the Mughals did not show much interest in Sikh activities. He acquired a piece of land on the left bank of the river Satluj in the principality of Hindour/Nalagar and founded Kiratpur (town of praise). At the time of his death, Guru Hargobind appointed Harirai (1630–61), one of his grandsons, as his successor, who later appointed a son, Harkishan (1656–64) to the office.

Away from the central Punjab, this was a period of weakening of the office of the Guru and of a general distress for the community. In addition to the external challenges detailed above, the community had also seen the rise of dissidence from within. Guru Nanak's son, Srichand was the first dissident. With his belief in a life of celibacy and detachment from the world, he failed to attract any support for himself within the Sikh fold, but he created a following known as the **Udasis** (the renunciants). This group was close to the Nath Yogis in its beliefs and practice and there is no contemporary evidence that it ever considered itself as part of the Sikh community. The Sikhs firmly rejected the doctrinal stance of the Udasis.

Later on, the sons of Guru Angad, Datu and Dasu, and of Guru Amardas, Mohan and Mohri, followed the earlier pattern and they challenged the appointed successors, forcing them to leave the existing seats of authority and build new centers. Unlike Srichand, these individuals did not have doctrinal differences with the larger Sikh community. In time, they made peace and offered allegiance to the court at Ramdaspur, and began to work closely with the leaders there.

Finally, the conflict between the sons and the successors became an internal family matter. Guru Ramdas's decision to elevate his youngest son, Arjan, as successor may have curtailed the problem of the shift of geographical location, but dissent continued to erupt. Guru Ramdas's elder son, Prithi Chand, did not accept his brother Arjan's authority. Guru Hargobind's eldest grandson, Dhirmal, challenged the appointment of his younger brother Harirai. Guru Harirai's eldest son, Ramrai, challenged the elevation of his brother Harkishan first, and then of his nominee, Tegh Bahadur (1621–75), as the ninth Guru. In this phase of conflict, the dissidents left the center and established their separate seats, Prithi Chand at Hehar, Dhirmal at Kartarpur, and Ramrai at Dehradun. Prithi Chand's descendants moved to Ramdaspur after Guru Hargobind's departure from there.

These seats of authority posed a challenge to Sikh belief in the unity of Guruship since all these people could not be considered legitimate leaders. With the exception of this multiplicity of succession, however, there were no other major doctrinal differences between the mainstream community and these alternative seats. They all evoked Guru Nanak's authority, shared the same scriptural text, prayers and rituals, and celebrated the same festivals. Their competition was centered on control over the institutional structures within the community. Dissidents were successful in winning the loyalty of some Masand families and the local resources that were available to them. Regarding their relationship with the administration, they all were beneficiaries of revenue-free grants, and occupied their seats with Mughal blessing.

Returning to the mainstream, Guru Harkishan at the time of his death nominated Tegh Bahadur, his grand uncle and the youngest son of Guru Hargobind, as his successor. Tegh Bahadur, which literally means "brave swordsman," was born in Ramdaspur and had spent the early years of his life in the comforts of the Sikh court there. At the time of his ascension to the high office, Guru Tegh Bahadur was the most widely traveled leader after the founder of the community and had good knowledge of Sikh congregations both in the Punjab plains and in distant towns.

In 1665, Guru Tegh Bahadur acquired Makhowal, a village in the valley ten miles toward the north of Kiratpur in the principality of Bilaspur, and in its vicinity founded Chak Nanaki (town of Nanaki), after his mother. Guru Tegh Bahadur was the first Guru after Guru Arjan to compose poetry, and he writes that an ideal person is he who does not frighten anyone and is afraid of no one (M9, GG, 1427), that liberation is a state of fearlessness (M9, GG, 632, 726, 830, 902), and that the use of physical force to rid oneself of shackles on the way to liberation is fully justified (M9, GG, 1429). The Sikh sacred text was updated and Guru Tegh Bahadur's compositions were added to the existing body of work.

At Chak Nanaki, the Guru focused on recreating the glory of the Sikh court of Ramdaspur. Guru Tegh Bahadur's extensive travels helped him tighten the ties between the center here and congregations in distant places. He also invited poets and patronized them at his court, and we see the Sikh center beginning to have the semblance of what the Guru must have seen at Ramdaspur during his childhood. The Guru also continued to go on tours and preach a message of fearlessness, which was interpreted as instigation for rebellion by the Mughals. In 1675, the Guru was arrested and publicly executed in Delhi. This second execution of a Guru stunned the community and paved the way for his son Gobind to reshape the destiny of his followers in fundamental ways.

Guru Gobind Singh

The only son of Guru Tegh Bahadur, Gobind, was born in Patna, in the present-day state of Bihar, during the travels of his father. He was brought to Chak Nanaki, Punjab, when he was six years old, taught Braj, Persian, and Punjabi, and trained in the use of arms and the tactics of war. Having become a leader during the tragic circumstances of his father's death, the Guru had the responsibility of consolidating the center, and of bringing the fragmented groups in central Punjab under his leadership.

The strengthening of the center at Chak Nanaki implied confrontation with Bhim Chand, the Rajput chief of Bilaspur, in whose territory the area fell. Tensions were inherent in the situation because the Sikhs claimed territorial autonomy while Bhim Chand considered them to be his vassals. As the tensions continued, the Guru decided to leave the town in 1685 and move to Paunta on the bank of the river Yamuna. However, Sikh success in battles with the Rajput chiefs in the Yamuna area boosted their confidence and they moved their center back to Chak Nanaki in 1688. In its vicinity, the Guru established a new town named Anandpur (town of ecstasy) and built a fort at each of its four corners. In the 1690s, the Sikh court at Anandpur flourished, with poets, and in all likelihood some painters, enjoying the Guru's patronage.

During this period of stability, Guru Gobind was able to attend to the needs of distant congregations. An increasing number of Sikhs began to visit Anandpur on festival days. This is reflected in the addition of a new festival, called Hola Mahala, which marked the end of winter, to the existing festivals of Vaisakhi and Divali. The visiting families brought their tithes with them and some stayed on for a while, which added to the vibrancy of life at Anandpur. In 1696, Guru Gobind also took over the control of the Darbar Sahib establishment. This was a result of the death of Hariji, the grandson of Prithi Chand, and the weakening of his family's authority in Ramdaspur.

At the end of the decade, a major event took place that was to have a profound impact on Sikh history. Guru Gobind declared the Sikhs to be the Khalsa, "the community of the pure" and answerable only to Vahiguru. This renaming or elevation was the most important moment in Sikh history after the birth of the founder. Writing in the 1940s, Teja Singh, the leading Sikh scholar of the period, presents the traditional account of the event as follows:

> On the Vaisakhi day of 1699 the Guru called a big meeting of his Sikhs at Anandpur and told them of his mission. At the end of his speech he drew out his sword and cried, "Is there anyone here who would lay down his life for religion?" At

this the whole assembly was thrown into consternation; but the Guru went on repeating his demand. At the third call Daya Ram, a Khatri of Lahore, rose from his seat and offered himself. The Guru took him into the adjoining enclosure, where a few goats were kept tied, and seating him there cut off a goat's head. He came out with a dripping weapon and, flourishing it before the multitude, asked them again, "Is there any other Sikh here who will offer himself as a sacrifice?" At this Dharm Das of Delhi, a Jaṭ, came forward and was taken into the enclosure, where another goat was killed. In the same way three other men stood up one after another and offered themselves for sacrifice. One was Muhkam Chand, a washerman of Dvarka; another was Himmat, a cook of Jagannath [Puri]; the third was Sahib Chand, a barber of Bidar. The Guru, after dressing the five in handsome clothes, brought them before the assembly. He baptized them with water stirred with a dagger and called them his beloved ones. He took the same baptism from them as a sign that he was one of them. . . They were taught to believe in Vahiguru and the mission of the Ten Gurus.

We also have early reports of Mata Jito, the Guru's wife, participating in the ceremony by adding "sugar lumps" to the spiritual mix and thereby making it fit for human consumption. (See page 41.)

The symbolism of the description is poignant. The declaration is constructed around the call for human sacrifice, which provided the Sikhs with a once-in-a-lifetime opportunity to affirm their loyalty to the tradition and community. Bhai Gurdas had already declared that a group of five Sikhs represented the presence of Vahiguru and, stemming from this belief, the Guru sought five Sikhs who could meet a higher level of dedication. Their names mentioned in the account—Daya (compassion), Dharm (duty), Muhkam (firmness), Himmat (effort), and Sahib (honor)—stand for a set of important Sikh values. These five individuals came from varied backgrounds, thus emphasizing the social comprehensiveness of Sikh appeal. The towns they came from—Bidar, Delhi, Dvarka, Lahore, and Jagannath Puri— were major centers of politics and religion in medieval India. The strength of this traditional account is found in its elaborate symbolism, which encourages heroism and exemplifies willingness to die in defense of one's religious tradition.

Preparation of the khande di pahul. Lahora Singh. Gouache on paper, late 19th century. Courtesy of Punjab Archives, Chandigarh.

Writing in 1711, Sainapati, a poet at the Anandpur court, reports the same event in less dramatic details but successfully brings its real significance to focus. He writes that on this historic day the Guru turned the total community into the Khalsa or the pure Sikhs (*sagal Sikh bhaai Khalsa*). Having assigned the community the name of the Khalsa, the Guru assured its liberation (*kiau nam khalas khalasi batai*). Chaupa Singh, another member of the Guru's court, also reports the turning of the total community (*sarbat sangat*) into the Khalsa.

What implications did this declaration carry? First, the Guru restructured the system of authority both within the community, as well as in its relationship to the external centers of power. With this declaration, the existing system of three-tiered authority, comprising the Masands (local deputies), the Guru, and the sacred scripture, was dissolved. The Guru eliminated the office of the Masands, and the congregations were told to establish direct contact with Anandpur and bring the tithe there themselves. The Guru also placed himself within the larger fold of the Khalsa, and thus initiated the process of the

dissolution of his office. In the past, the Guru (as an authority figure) had been an easy target for the Mughals, and the office had
also been the cause of internal dissentions. The Guru appealed to
his rivals in other seats also to renounce their authority and to
unify the communal resources.

With the personal authority of the Guru formally eliminated, Sikh
scripture, the repository of revelation, moved to the center of the
structure of authority within the Khalsa. As already observed, the Sikh
sacred text had originated with Guru Nanak and was updated as
the later Gurus' compositions became available. The absence of the
authoritative signature of Nanak in the compositions attributed to the
tenth Guru, and his decision not to incorporate them into the earlier sacred work implied that the revelation was by definition complete.
This had a two-fold implication: first, the existing text had reached
canonical status, and, second, the presence of a personal Guru, the
primary medium of revelation to the Sikhs, was no longer necessary.

For the contemporary poet Sainapati, Vahiguru was the Khalsa's
only patron, and in turn, the Khalsa was elevated to be the chosen
instrument of divine victory. The Khalsa was assigned a clearly defined
mission of punishing evil (*asur singharbe*) and establishing Sikh sovereignty (Satigur da Raj). Rooted in this is the belief that the struggle
of the Khalsa did not simply enjoy divine approval; rather, the Khalsa
itself is divine in nature because it is executing divine justice on earth.
Since Guru Nanak sang of Vahiguru as the destroyer of evil (M1,
GG, 138), the Khalsa was to execute the divine will in the world.

In order to prepare members of the Khalsa to accomplish this
specific goal, Sainapati reports that the Guru now introduced the
khande di pahul (nectar of the double-edged sword) ritual. Chaupa
Singh explains important details of the original ceremony. The
making of the nectar involved the recitation of sacred Sikh compositions over water stirred with the sword. After the ritual drinking
of the nectar, the individual made the public declaration that the Khalsa
belonged to Vahiguru (*Vahiguru ji ka Khalsa*), and its role was to fight
for divine victory on this earth (*Vahiguru ji ki fateh*). Finally, the original five to undergo the ceremony were assigned the authority to
administer the *khande di pahul* to others.

The title **Singh** (lion), a marker of nobility, was appended to
the name of the individual who took part in the ceremony as Guru
Gobind himself did and thus became Guru Gobind Singh. (See page

Guru Gobind Singh. Gouache on paper, circa 1700. *

43.) This formal addition to the name marked the rise of a group within the Sikh community that was dedicated to the communal goals and was willing to work for them, like the first five, at the expense of their lives if required. Guru Nanak's conception of a life of honor and fearlessness thus found its embodiment in the Singhs.

For Chaupa Singh, with the turning of the community into the Khalsa, the existing Rahit centered on the belief in the unity of Vahiguru, congregational worship, and a life of moral and social commitment (*dharm di kirat*) was expanded to include working toward the establishment of the Khalsa Raj and carrying a set of external symbols (*bahar di nishani*). The general expectation was that the Singhs, those who had undergone the *khande di pahul*, would follow the Rahit in its entirety, while the rest of the community would do so to the best of its ability.

In the expanded Rahit, Guru Nanak's emphasis on the purity of the body and the need to keep it clean took interesting concrete forms. To keep the body in its pristine form, an injunction was issued against the shaving of bodily hair (**kes**). The hair on the head was to be kept clean, obliging the Sikhs to carry a comb (**kangha**), and was also to be covered in a neatly tied turban, which bestowed on them a visible appearance generally associated with royalty. Along with this, the Sikhs were to wear a pair of britches (**kachha**), understood to be part of a warrior's dress. The tradition of carrying arms that was popular in the 1690s became an obligation to wear "five arms," which included a sword (**kirpan**), and a steel bracelet to protect the wrist (**kara**), among others.

In the years following the declaration of the Khalsa, Sainapati reports that the Sikh center at Anandpur thrived (*Satigur Raj chahu dis bhayo*). However, the political assertiveness of the Sikhs was seen as a direct challenge to the authority of the hill chiefs, who in early 1704 sought the support of Emperor Aurangzeb, and he instructed the Mughal governor at Sirhind to help them. In a joint front, they put a siege around Anandpur, forcing the Sikhs to vacate it in December 1704. In the confusion that followed the evacuation, the elder sons of Guru Gobind Singh, Ajit Singh and Jujhar Singh, died fighting, and Zoravar Singh and Fateh Singh, the younger ones, along with Mata Gujari, the Guru's mother, were captured. The children were later executed under the orders of the governor of Sirhind, and Mata Gujari died in prison.

Guru Gobind Singh wrote a letter to Emperor Aurangzeb complaining of this unjust treatment and while he was in Talvandi Sabo, Bhatinda, the Guru received the emperor's invitation to meet him. Before the meeting could take place, however, the emperor died and in the battle for the succession, the Guru blessed Prince Muazam. After the prince became Emperor Bahadur Shah (r. 1707–12), the Guru accompanied him to South India, where he became the target of an assassination and died in 1708. In his short life, Guru Gobind Singh radically restructured the authority within the Sikh (Khalsa) community, and at the same time provided it with a vision for its future. In accomplishing this, he carved a place for himself in Sikh history that is considered second only to that of the founder of the tradition.

Establishing the Khalsa Raj

Sainapati concludes his touching account of Guru Gobind Singh's death with an aside that refers to the community's concern about succession. The Guru's emphatic answer was that he bestows "his mantle on the Khalsa," and will remain eternally united with it. In addition, "the eternal word" will be the true guide. In actual terms, the community is elevated to the status of the **Guru Panth**, and the scriptural text, which by now was known as the Adi Granth (original book), to that of the **Guru Granth** (the Guru in book form). The antecedents of the centrality of the text can be traced back to the inception of the community, and the phasing out of the office of the Guru had started with the declaration of the Khalsa.

The absence of the Guru was compounded by the loss of the communal center after the evacuation of Anandpur. The guiding hand to fill this void seems to have been that of Bhai Mani Singh (d. 1738), a leading scribe of the times, and an authority on Sikh beliefs and history, whose death was celebrated in *Shahidbilas* (splendor of martyrdom), composed in 1802. After Guru Gobind Singh's death, Bhai Mani Singh, based at the Darbar Sahib, began to work toward positioning it as the center of Sikh sacred geography. Built by Guru Arjan, it had considerable name-recognition, and being situated in the heartland of the Sikh community it was easily accessible. (See map above.) Bhai Mani Singh revived the tradition of Sikhs visiting the Darbar Sahib

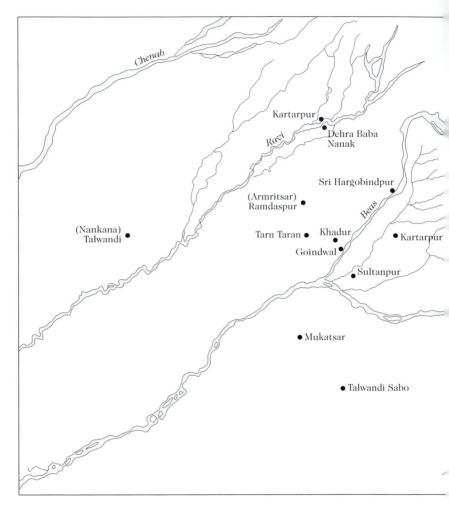

regularly as well as on the festival days of Vaisakhi and Divali. While these festivals introduced vibrancy to Sikh religious life, they also provided the Darbar Sahib with economic stability in the form of tithes.

The Vaisakhi and Divali meetings at the Darbar Sahib also created the context for collective reflection on issues confronting the community. We see at this time the affirmation of a belief that whenever the Khalsa gathers in the presence of the Guru Granth, the mystic attendance of the personal Guru is with them, elevating the

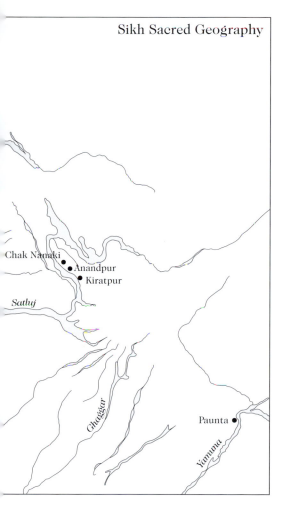

Sikh Sacred Geography

assembly to the status of the Guru Panth or the community as the Guru. In this situation, whatever decision the assembly reached was considered the Guru's will (**gurmata**), and morally binding on all Sikhs irrespective of whether they were actually present at the event. When a major decision was to be taken, an effort was made to invite the community from far and near to come to the Darbar Sahib on the day appointed and this was considered the meeting of the total community (*sarbat khalsa*).

While Bhai Mani Singh was working out the institutional structures to meet the needs of the time, another religio-political development within the framework of the Khalsa ideology was unfolding on the eastern edge of the Punjab. As part of Guru Gobind Singh's plan to return to Anandpur, he had commissioned Banda Singh (1670–1716), a follower at Nander, to go to the Punjab, organize the community, and wait for the Guru's return. After the Guru's death, Banda Singh viewed his mission in broader terms as waging war against the Mughals and establishing the Khalsa Raj. The Sikhs in the Punjab received him as the bearer of the last command of the Guru and offered him their full support.

Under the leadership of Banda Singh, the Sikhs began their political ascendancy in the eastern Punjab, and were able eventually to capture Sirhind in May 1710. In the following months, they went on the offensive, traveling to the west across the rivers Satluj, Beas, and Ravi, and to the east across the river Yamuna. It took three successive Mughal emperors to contain the challenge posed by the Sikhs. Banda Singh along with several hundred Sikhs was besieged and eventually captured in the upper Bari Doab. The prisoners were taken to Delhi and publicly executed in 1716. The Mughals may have thought that the Sikh threat had finally come to an end but for the Sikhs it was just the beginning of the struggle.

The Khalsa ideology that fired the Sikh imagination was centered on the belief that they were to supplant an illegitimate rule and herald a new era. This was marked by a new set of symbols: a new capital city at Mukhlispur (city of the purified), a new official seal, new coins, a new calendar, a new insignia, and a new flag (**Nishan Sahib**). The inscriptions on the seal and the coins indicate that Banda Singh regarded the ultimate authority as being vested with Vahiguru who had come to the Sikhs through the grace of the Gurus. The insignia of *degh tegh fateh* (cauldron, sword, victory) marked the commitment to feed the hungry and provide justice to all in the Khalsa Raj. (See page 49.)

Based on a principle of justice, the Sikhs were not to permit harassment of the common people (*khalaq*). The Mughal records refer to the violence and destruction that followed the Sikh attack on Sirhind. However, the fact remains that the important Muslim religious sites, such as the Lal Masjid, the tombs of Ustad and Shagird, and the Am-Khas Bagh, were all left untouched. Also, for the followers

Degh tegh fateh. The text of the Jap is inscribed within it. 19th century. Courtesy of Guru Nanak Dev University, Amritsar, Punjab.

of Guru Nanak, for whom nature reflected the divine immanence (M1, GG, 580), pillage or burning of the fields, a common practice of their enemies, was not allowed.

A composition popular in the 1710s, which continues to be part of current Sikh prayers, reiterates the Khalsa's destiny to rule (***raj karega khalsa***). This community's political success, no matter how short lived, was thus emblazoned in the Sikh imagination. With Banda Singh's death, Sikh communal activity became centered in Ramdaspur. Relationships with the Mughal authorities continued hostile. Nadir Shah's invasion of the region in 1738, followed by Ahmad Shah Durrani's annexation of the Punjab to his Afghan empire, provided a fertile ground for Sikh chiefs to assert their power

*Ranjit Singh. Jivan Ram. Lithograph of water color and pencil original, 1831.**

and carve territories for themselves, both in the central Punjab and in the Malwa. When the Sikh flag was raised in Lahore in 1765, the dream of the Khalsa Raj took a concrete form.

Toward the end of the century, Ranjit Singh emerged as the most talented leader. He was able to bring under his control large areas in the Punjab plains and thought it logical to extend his domain to the Malwa and subvert the Sikh chiefs there. The Malwa chiefs, however, preferred to seek protection from the British, who by this time had replaced the Mughal power in the subcontinent and had expanded their area of direct influence to the river Yamuna. This brought Ranjit Singh and the British into confrontation, but the situation was amicably resolved with the Treaty of Amritsar in 1809, in which the British recognized Ranjit Singh as the sovereign ruler to the north of the river Satluj.

Once the southern boundary was set, Ranjit Singh subjugated the chiefs in the hills, and took Multan (1818), Kashmir (1819), and a large area across the Indus from the control of the Afghans. To train the Khalsa army, Ranjit Singh hired European officers, several of whom had served under Napoleon Bonaparte. From the 1830s onward, the soldiers had drills in the morning, wore uniforms, and were awarded medals. The Sikhs consolidated the Punjab in an unprecedented manner, and the 186-carat diamond known as the Kohinoor, once the precious possession of the Mughal, the Iranian, and then the Afghan rulers, now adorned the right arm of their leader, Ranjit Singh.

Nationalistic aspirations

Despite the difficulties of the period, it brought some important ideas and nationalistic aspirations into focus. Earlier, Sainapati had sung of the death of Ajit Singh, one of Guru Gobind Singh's sons, as a martyrdom which resulted in his attaining liberation and becoming an object of reverence for the Sikhs. Writing in 1751, Koer Singh had claimed that the martyrdom of 125,000 Sikhs was necessary before their political supremacy could be established, and many seemed ready to offer their lives toward this cause. Now, with the establishment of political power in the Punjab, the myth of the divine origin of Sikh political authority was promulgated. The inscriptions on the Sikh coins attributed sovereignty to Guru Nanak and Guru Gobind Singh, and a story of the time tells how Guru Gobind Singh had blessed the Sikhs with the land of the Punjab to rule. According to this story, the Guru actually encouraged the Sikhs to inhabit other areas but they wanted to stay only in central Punjab (Majha).

The Sikh rationale for the pursuit of political power had originated in a context in which first the Mughals and then the Rajputs were believed to have infringed upon Sikh autonomy and their right to live with dignity. In the early eighteenth century, therefore, the Sikhs declared that both the Rajputs and the Mughals represented evil. According to this view, the Rajputs started the problems at Anandpur and were thus responsible for what followed. The eighteenth-century Rahit documents denounce religious leaders and practices of both Hindus and Muslims. Later in the century, however, as the new rulers of the region, the Sikhs were to execute justice and be responsible for "the welfare of the all" (*sarbat da bhala*). The "benevolent monarchy" of Ranjit Singh protected the common people, irrespective of their religious beliefs, and incorporated both the Rajputs and the Mughals into the ruling elite. Being pragmatic people, the Sikhs accepted Lahore as their political center and permitted the Persian language to continue as the language of administration.

As it had a non-proselytizing tradition, the Sikh community made no effort to attract new recruits, but the urban Sikhs who were unable to cope with the Mughal persecution later became comfortable and began openly to practice a Sikh way of life. The number of Sikhs among the rural population also seems to have grown. The literature of the period indicates that Sikh belief and practice underwent considerable elaboration, and a set of complex rituals to show reverence to the Guru Granth was formulated. A reading of the complete text became part of Sikh devotional practices. Sarup Singh Koushish, a late eighteenth-century writer, mentions the tradition of the performance of an unbroken reading (*akhaṇḍ paṭh*) of the Guru Granth at the time of Guru Gobind Singh's departure from Talvandi Sabo to meet the Mughal emperor. The Sikh identification with Punjabi and the Gurmukhi script was consolidated. The script was to be treated with respect (*adab*), and sheets of papers, which had Gurmukhi letters recorded on them, were not to be utilized for mundane purposes.

In addition to being a place of worship, the gurdwara (Guru's house) emerged as a marker of Sikh sacred history. As will be seen in Chapter 4, the definition of the gurdwara extended to cover Sikh historic sites associated with the Gurus as well as later events in Sikh history. The Darbar Sahib regained its earlier status as the center of the Sikh sacred geography, followed by four sites: the Akal Takhat in the Darbar Sahib precincts, the Harimandir Sahib, Patna, the Kesgar Sahib, Anandpur, and the Hazur Sahib, Nander. While the Akal Takhat is associated with Guru Hargobind, the latter three are associated with Guru Gobind Singh, marking respectively the place of his birth, the declaration of the Khalsa, and his death. All four would eventually emerge as the **Takhats** (thrones or centers of authority).

New gurdwaras were erected on other sites. By the early nineteenth century, the Punjabi landscape was studded with buildings that marked sacred Sikh sites. This extensive construction provided a venue for service, as Sikh chiefs contributed through their resources and the lay Sikhs through their labor. With the population of Ramdaspur topping 100,000, the town became the most populous in the region and began increasingly to be called Amritsar after "the pool of nectar" at its center.

There were voices raised in protest against some developments within the community. Writing in 1769, Kesar Singh Chhibbar complained that love for temporal power was taking the Sikhs away from their religious beliefs. Some decades later, **Baba** Dayal (d. 1855) felt unhappy with those Sikhs who continued to visit the Hindu temples and associate with their priests. In time he developed a following, known as the **Nirankaris**, from among the urban trading communities in the northwest Punjab. Balak Singh (1799–1862) and later his disciple Ram Singh (1816–1885) did not like the fact that some Sikhs were participating in the worship of tombs and cremation sites, and publicly called for these places to be destroyed. Their followers came from among the **Ramgarias** (carpenters/Tarkhans) and are called the **Namdharis**.

In conclusion, after Guru Gobind Singh's death we see the authority of the personal Guru moving on to the Guru Granth, and the Guru Panth attaining the right to take decisions on behalf of the community. Early in the eighteenth century, Chaupa Singh claimed that the Sikhs were like a mote in the eyes of "the Hindus and the Muslims." Their numbers may have been small but their existence was established. For Gurdas Singh, writing in the second half of the eighteenth century, the Sikhs represented the "third religion" (*tisar mazhab*), which was "clearly superior" to those of the Hindus and the

Muslims. By the mid-nineteenth century, the Sikhs saw themselves as a *qaum* (which is a Persian term for a community with connotations of a nation), which stood among others like the "Mount Sumer," a mythological point from where the creation was said to have begun. The Sikhs constituted a thriving political elite who believed that they ruled the land of the Punjab on behalf of their Gurus and Vahiguru. The next chapter examines how the loss of power and the winds of modernity had an impact on the Sikh community.

To trace the evolution of the Sikh community in the modern period, the chapter is divided into four sections. In the first two sections, the Sikh community's encounter with the British and the impact of modern institutions, such as Western education and systems of governance, on Sikh life are examined. In the third section, the focus is on Sikh life in the Punjab after the departure of the British and the independence of the sub-continent. In the fourth section, the Sikh migration to different parts of India and beyond is traced. In the process, Sikh appropriation of modern modes of thinking into everyday life and the problems that have presented themselves are analyzed.

The arrival of the British

In the mid-nineteenth century, the thriving city of Amritsar with the Darbar Sahib at its public center symbolized the community's religious as well as temporal well-being. After the destruction of its original precinct by the Afghans in the 1750s, the Sikhs rebuilt the Darbar Sahib and the Akal Takhat in its vicinity with the best materials and expertise available in the region. Ranjit Singh had commissioned the embellishing of the buildings with marble inlay, and gold-plated the domes. The interior of the Darbar Sahib with its abundance of floral designs in red, blue and gold was the artistic replication of the Sikh claim in the 1540s that radiance falls around the Guru's seat (GG, 967).

After the death of Ranjit Singh in 1839, it became increasingly clear that his successors did not have his abilities to direct the destiny of the Sikh kingdom. The British had subjugated the subcontinent and were, by this time, entrenched on the banks of the river Satluj.

In the conflict that ensued, they destroyed Sikh military power in 1846, and formally annexed the Sikh kingdom in 1849.

The annexation of the Punjab came at a very high price, for the number of British officers killed while defeating the Sikhs was equivalent to the total number of British lives lost in bringing the rest of the subcontinent under control. The Sikhs were in utter disarray, wondering how they could lose their divinely ordained sovereignty. The fact that their defeat came at the hands of the Purabias (soldiers from eastern India, who constituted the majority of the British army and for whose fighting ability Sikhs had utter disdain) made it even more painful to accept. Thus the early phase of the Sikh–British relationship was defined by feelings of mutual hostility and resentment.

In early 1857, however, a group of north Indian soldiers in the British army rebelled, captured Delhi, and declared Bahadur Shah II, a Mughal descendent, the emperor of the country. The Malwa Sikh chiefs supported the British, but that did not seem enough. Faced with a difficult situation, the British called on the former Khalsa army for help. Sikh soldiers responded positively and viewed the occasion as an opportunity to settle their old scores with the Purabias and the Mughals. With their help, the British crushed the mutiny.

This development started a phase of close cooperation between the Sikhs and British. The British restored the privileges of Sikh nobility and assigned them the status of honorary magistrates. They also acknowledged the gurdwara custodians as Sikh religious leaders and settled large portions of the gurdwara endowments on their personal names. The British opened the doors of their army and the Sikhs joined in great numbers. To enable Sikhs to make a smooth transition into British army life, the British permitted the traditions of the Khalsa army, such as wearing the turban and taking the *khaṇḍe di pahul*, to continue. The British interest in the economic development of the Punjab further cemented this relationship.

This Sikh–British cooperation, however, began slowly to erode at the beginning of the twentieth century. The British had made efforts toward accommodating Indians in running affairs of state, and were interested in working out a system based on communal representation. The Punjab was the only state that, in addition to a small number of Jains and Christians, contained three major religious communities—Muslims (over 50 per cent), Hindus (under 40 per cent), and Sikhs (less than 10 per cent)—and the region defied any system of governance proposed for the rest of the country. There was also a fundamental division between the British criterion of representation based on numbers and the Sikh leadership's expectation that it correspond with the size of their financial contribution to the state treasury and their services in the army.

Another religio-legal tangle also became a source of considerable conflict. For the Sikhs, the gurdwaras had always been communal institutions, and not the personal property of their custodians: a position that the British were aware of but had overlooked while settling the gurdwara properties in revenue records. By late 1910, Sikh leadership disapproved of the practices of some of the gurdwara custodians, and expected the British to remove them. The British interpreted the demand as an issue concerning property rights, and as such to be settled by the courts. Sikh leadership was not prepared to get into these prolonged litigations. This resulted in a confrontation, which according to the information presented at the Punjab Legislative Council, involved "400 deaths, 2,000 wounded, 30,000 arrests, and five million rupees' worth of fines." The problem was eventually resolved with the passage of the Gurdwara Reform Act in 1925.

The struggle over ownership of the gurdwaras helped the emergence of the Akali Dal (the army of the Immortal One), which considered itself responsible for protecting the political interests of the Sikh community. After 1925, when it became clear that the British would eventually have to leave India, the Akali Dal leadership was divided about how best to secure a stable future for the community. At all critical junctures, some wanted to continue supporting the British with the expectation that they would allow the creation of a Sikh state before they left, while others thought that working with the Indian National Congress, a political party fighting for the independence of India, would be beneficial in the long run. While the Akali Dal and its various groups represented the majority of Sikhs, both the Congress Party and the Communist Party of India were also able to build a support base among the Sikhs.

The Sikhs fought with the Allied forces in both World War I and II with casualties numbering "83,005 soldiers killed and 109,045 wounded." Despite vehement opposition from the Congress party, the Akali Dal supported the British in World War II, and, in turn, expected the British to protect Sikh interests. The Akali Dal's official position was that if India was going to be divided to meet the demand of the Muslim League's leadership, a separate state should be created for the Sikhs in the central Punjab and the Sikhs should have the right to federate with either Hindustan or Pakistan. This view was tied to the belief that the Sikhs constituted a separate community and therefore should not be forced to live within either a Hindu or a Muslim majority. The separate state was envisioned as Khalistan (country of the Khalsa), a sovereign Sikh state, and was formally demanded in 1940 and 1944.

Given the demographic situation, however, the Akali Dal leaders could not make a convincing case for a separate Sikh state and were left with no option but to cast their lot with India. The Punjab was vivisected and 60 per cent of the area went to the newly created state of Pakistan. The ensuing migration of eight million people crossing the border in opposite directions was blighted by violence that left around 300,000 people dead. So, in 1947, as India entered a new era of freedom under the leadership of Jawaharlal Nehru (1885–1964), and Pakistan was establishing a new future under Mohammad Ali Jinnah (1876–1948), the Punjab and the Sikhs became the epicenter of bloody violence.

The beginning of the modern era

The British brought with them to the Punjab a variety of innovations: a new legal system, Western education, census taking, urban forms, and so on. The values of human equality and dignity on which these institutions were built were not entirely new to the Sikhs but their guises were unfamiliar. While these institutions opened new arenas of knowledge, the newspapers and the printing press also introduced unprecedented means of spreading information.

Sikh leadership responded to the new developments in diverse ways. At one extreme we find Baba Ram Singh, the Namdhari leader (see p. 53), who categorically rejected the way of life that came with the British. At the other was Dayal Singh Majithia (1849–98), a Sikh aristocrat educated in the Christian Missionary School, Amritsar, who became an unequivocal supporter of modernity, and vehemently argued that indigenous modes of knowledge must be supplanted by Western education.

The broad Sikh leadership rejected the Namdhari stance of resistance and gave a qualified support to Dayal Singh's enthusiastic embrace of modernity. Their guiding principle was that the Sikhs needed to participate fully in the new institutions, while keeping their heritage firmly intact. The arrival of the printing press in Lahore, for instance, was welcomed. The first lithograph edition of the Guru Granth was published in 1865 and, during the next twenty years, eleven different editions and reprints were released. Although Punjabi written in Gurmukhi was the Sikh sacred language, there was no resistance to the Guru Granth being translated and published in English.

Sikh leadership also warmly received the arrival of Western learning into the Punjab. The Khalsa College was set up in 1892 in a building designed by Ram Singh (1857–1916), a Sikh architect, and its impressive structure on the periphery of Amritsar, symbolized the entry of the Sikh community into the modern world. A public appeal to contribute toward its construction was issued at the Akal Takhat. Sikh nobles contributed funds, and the Sikhs in the surrounding villages offered their free labor. Here, the students were to be trained in areas such as the sciences and English literature, while being thoroughly grounded in their Sikh heritage. A gurdwara stood at the center of the campus, where students met for morning and evening prayers, and a separate curriculum was created to teach Sikh history and religion. In 1894, Bhai Takhat Singh (1870–1937) opened a boarding school for women at Ferozepure. These institutions were seen as places where Sikhs could be educated in the ways of modern learning.

The arrival of the British also brought new elements to the religious life of the Punjab. With them came Christian missionaries and the Brahmo Samajis, a Hindu reform movement, that worked hard to establish a foothold in the region. The Punjabi Muslims created Anjumans (associations) to initiate reflection, and Mirza Gulam Ahmad (1839–1908), the founder of the Ahmadiyah movement in Islam, took active part in these discussions. Swami Dayanand (1824–83), the founder of the Arya Samaj, another Hindu reform movement, visited Lahore in 1877 and contributed significantly to this ferment.

As far as the Sikhs were concerned, there was an additional reason for anxiety. From the 1850s the census reports had indicated that the Sikhs constituted less than ten per cent of the Punjabi population and that they were not in a majority anywhere in the region. Hindu leadership's unprecedented assertion that Sikhs were a part of their fold further heightened these concerns. The claim may have had a degree of legitimacy regarding the urban Sikhs—some of whom had maintained marital ties with Hindu society—but it had no relevance for over 90 per cent of the Sikh population. This vehement claim by the Hindus was aimed at raising Hindu community numbers to equal those of the Muslims.

Doctrinal debates

As discussed earlier (see p. 53), voices like that of Baba Dayal had already expressed discomfort at the way some Sikhs practiced their beliefs. Post-British developments initiated formal reflections on these issues. In 1873, Sikh leaders met in Amritsar and founded the **Singh Sabha** (Society of the Singhs), which was later registered under the Joint Stock Companies Act of 1860. Khem Singh Bedi (1832–1905), a descendent of Guru Nanak, was one of its leading figures. The second Singh Sabha was started in Lahore in 1879 with Gurmukh Singh (1849–98), a teacher at Oriental College, Lahore, at the forefront. Another Singh Sabha was established at Bhasaur in 1893 with Teja Singh Bhasaur (1867–1933) as its leader.

As the name suggests, the "Singhs" were seen to constitute the nucleus of the community, but the need was felt to delineate the finer details of belief and practice, the relationship of various phases of history, and the status and position of the groups at the community's periphery. The period of **Rahitnamas** (manuals of Rahit) had given way to print media with large circulation, and the new situation demanded a clear position on the above-mentioned issues. From the debates that followed, three positions emerged.

Khem Singh Bedi represented one point of view. To understand his ideological position, some biographical information is useful. Being a descendent of Guru Nanak, he considered himself a guru, and largely modeled his role after Guru Gobind Singh. His biographers recognize his contribution to Sikh society in the areas of administering the *khande di pahul* to his followers and starting Sikh educational institutions. His personal following, however, included Sikh as well as Hindu Khatris living around his center in the northwest of Punjab. Avtar Singh Vahiria, whom Bedi employed to present his ideological position, supported the centrality of the Singh identity and the significance of the *khaṇḍe di pahul*, but he also argued in support of the idea of divine incarnation, the need for a living guru, and the indivisibility of Sikh and Hindu society.

Gurmukh Singh stood in the middle and represented the position that the activities of the ten Gurus and the Guru Granth serve as the ultimate source of Sikh belief and practice. The Guru Panth had the formal authority to interpret the Guru Granth. The Singh identity was ideal but those who had not undergone the *khaṇḍe di pahul* were an indivisible part of the Khalsa as long as they recognized the Guru Granth. Since the Sikhs constituted a distinct community, the nature of Hindu–Sikh relationship was a redundant issue. Gurmukh Singh was cognizant of the need for an authoritative statement of Sikh beliefs and their synchronization with prevalent practices.

Teja Singh Bhasaur represented the third position, which was also centered on the authority of the Guru Granth and the Guru Panth, but his general orientation to these issues was far more radical. He argued that the core of the Guru Granth was the compositions of the Gurus, and that the writings of others, such as the court poets and the non-Sikh saints, should have no place in Sikh scripture. Furthermore, Bhasaur claimed that any Sikh who had not undergone the *khaṇḍe di pahul* should have no place within the community. In his vision of "orthodoxy," the periphery was to be simply excised, and raising the issue of a Hindu–Sikh relationship was an insult to the Sikhs.

In order to understand the ideological outcome of this debate, we must look at some specific instances. First, the emphasis of Khem Singh Bedi on the *khaṇḍe di pahul* and the Singh way of life had full support from others, but his perception of a special status of "guru" for himself and his resistance to separating out his personal following into Sikhs and Hindus were not acceptable. It was argued that there is no provision for a "living guru" after the death of Guru Gobind Singh, and the very idea of divine incarnation flies in the face of Sikh belief. Building on the late eighteenth-century tradition of discomfort with the concept of descendents of the Gurus posing as gurus, Gurmukh Singh openly challenged Bedi's perception of personal authority.

Sikh conduct

Sources at the start of the eighteenth century mention external symbols of Sikh belief, such as the uncut hair (*kes*), the comb (*kangha*), wearing a pair of britches (*kachha*), and the five weapons that a Singh must always carry on him. By the end of the eighteenth century, these external symbols were coordinated with the Sikh symbolism surrounding the number five, and for Sarup Singh Koushish these five items included a comb (*kangha*), a small turban to cover the hair (*keski*), a bracelet (*karha*), a sword (*kirpan*), and a pair of britches (*kachha*). During the late nineteenth century, this set of five items was assigned its final form to include *kes*, *kangha*, *karha*, *kirpan*, and *kachha*, and was named the five ks, based on each item starting with the letter "k" in Punjabi, and carrying them was made absolutely obligatory. It is correct to note that the final systematization of these items and their name (five ks) were agreed during this period, but it is also important to remember that all these items (along with others) and their coordination with the Sikh symbolism of five had been in use long before this period.

A look at the Sikh marriage ceremony is of interest in this discussion. It is curious that while accounts of birth and death ceremonies begin early in the tradition, the first reference to marriage appears in *Sikhan di Bhagatmala* (rosary of Sikh devotees), a late eighteenth-century source attributed to Bhai Mani Singh. This brief reference says that Sikhs should perform their marriage by reciting Guru Amardas's *Anand* (ecstasy) and that Hindu priests should not be allowed to attend the ceremony.

Written in the 1820s, *Prem Sumarg* (path of love) provides us with the first detailed account of the Sikh marriage ceremony. A Sikh who is well versed in sacred literature oversees the ceremony and it is performed on a platform covered by a canopy that is held aloft by four spears. A sword stands at its center, and a small fire is made at its northern edge. As the ceremony begins, the bride walks over the fire and is offered the *khaṇḍe di pahul*, while the man is assumed to have already undertaken it. The bride and the groom communicate their agreement to marry. The congregation then asks in a prayer to Vahiguru for the well-being of the couple; this is repeated seven times, and at each completion *ghee* (clarified butter) is thrown on the fire. The women present in the congregation recite the *Anand*, and the **karhah prashad** (blessed food) is distributed with the bride and the groom feeding each other. This ceremony was also applicable for remarriage after widowhood.

Finally, references to the literature of the followers of Baba Dayal reveal that in 1808 he was married with recitation from the Guru Granth and without the presence of fire at the ceremony. We also have evidence of a public marriage performed in 1855, during which the Guru Granth was placed at the center, and the bride and the groom walked around it four times while one stanza each of Guru Ramdas's *Lavan* (circumambulations) was recited. It was followed by the recitation of the *Anand* and the supplication.

It is not known if this was the first marriage performed this way, nor is there comprehensive information about the precise situation in the larger community. The references above appear to describe the ceremony as performed among the urban Sikhs, with the role of fire, although considerably diminished, a continuation of the ceremony of pre-Sikh days, which has then been blended with Sikh elements. There is no information about the ceremony employed by the overwhelming majority of Sikhs who never had access to the fire ceremony. The late nineteenth-century Sikh leadership found the existing ceremony popular among the Nirankaris closest to the Sikh spirit and endorsed it.

Gurmukh Singh's position achieved acceptance, both in institutional and ideological terms. Kahn Singh Nabha (1861–1938), a scholar immersed in traditional Sikh learning, became its influential spokesperson. Quoting a wide variety of early Sikh sources, he generated a detailed statement of Sikh beliefs, practices, and political issues. In his writings, Nabha did not say anything fundamentally new, but the clarity with which he stated this position set him apart from earlier writers. Bedi and Bhasaur were eventually sidelined. Bedi died in 1905, and Bhasaur ended up being excommunicated in 1928 for tinkering with the canonical text of the Guru Granth.

The Chief Khalsa Diwan, a central organization based in Amritsar, played an important role in obtaining the legal sanction for Sikh ceremonies and propagating Sikh education. With the crucial help of Ripudaman Singh, the ruler of Nabha, the Anand Marriage Act legalizing the Sikh ceremony was passed in 1909. A new generation of scholars such as Bhai Vir Singh (1872–1957) and Teja Singh (1894–1958) made significant contributions toward the codification of Sikh ceremonies, editing of earlier Sikh texts, and setting the trend of incorporating new literary genres in creative writings in Punjabi.

The Gurdwaras

After World War I, gurdwara-related issues came into focus. To understand the situation, it is necessary to go back a little and reconnect
with the Udasis, who were the followers of Srichand (see p. 37). As
stated earlier, Guru Gobind Singh's declaration of the Khalsa was
geared toward containing the dissension within the Sikh fold. The
absence of any reference to the Udasis in the writings of both Sainapati and Chaupa Singh is an indication that they were not considered
part of the Sikh community.

During the persecution of the Sikhs in the early eighteenth
century, however, the Udasis established themselves in some gurdwaras and began to oversee their maintenance. This seems to have
come about because of the notional relationship they had with the
Sikhs, since they were the descendents of the followers of Guru Nanak's
son. With Sikh political ascendancy, the Udasis continued as the custodians of these places, where they largely followed Sikh beliefs
and practices. However, the situation underwent radical change under
the British revenue settlements. With the properties in their names,
these Udasis had the opportunity to build up their personal leadership and then assert their independence by disregarding the Sikh
norms in the gurdwaras under their control. This coincided with
the Hindu leadership's efforts to present the Sikh community as
part of their fold.

With the debates about the rejection of personal authority and
the need for coordination between belief and practice in the background, the Udasi situation became increasingly unacceptable to Sikh
leadership. The British treatment of the issue as a law and order problem generated a confrontation, which culminated in the Gurdwara
Act of 1925, and the creation of the Shiromani Gurdwara Prabandhak Committee (SGPC) or Supreme Gurdwara Management Committee
to oversee the management of the historic gurdwaras.

With its headquarters based in the precincts of the Darbar Sahib,
the SGPC, an elected body of the Sikhs, was called the Sikh parliament and was understood to constitute the modern version of the
Guru Panth. The management work required a consolidated statement of the Rahit in order to standardize the devotional practices
in the gurdwaras. A sub-committee of twenty-five scholars and
Sikh savants was set up, whose job was to consider the textual sources
and solicit views from individuals and organizations in order to

draft a report. The project took over twenty years to complete, and the resulting document, the *Rahit Maryada* (Sikh religious belief and practice) codified Sikh beliefs and established rituals on occasions such as birth, marriage, and death. It was published in 1950. The SGPC also created a standard edition of the Guru Granth. The lengthy process involved debates over the issue of the original manuscript, and how the earlier writing could best be presented in print. The committee also took on the responsibility of publishing different editions of the text for ceremonial and scholarly use.

As the British prepared to leave in 1947, the Sikhs as a religious community had negotiated well and made effective use of modern institutions. They had prepared a standard edition of Guru Granth, authoritative statements of history and beliefs, and were on their way to creating a manual of Rahit. They had worked out a democratic system in which both men and women voted to elect the members of the SGPC. Finally, they had built a chain of schools and colleges, where both Western education and Sikh heritage were taught.

Yet as a religious community with a firm belief in the organic relationship between religion and politics, the Sikhs found themselves in an awkward situation. Unlike the Indian Muslims, the Sikhs failed to make a case for a separate state. Sikh leaders in the Congress Party are often portrayed as "secularists" with religion playing no significant role in their politics, but it may be more accurate to see them as pragmatists, protecting Sikh interests within the framework of contemporary political realities. As for the Akali Dal leadership, since their main office was based in the precincts of the Darbar Sahib, separating religion and politics was never an option. In any case, the modern democratic system forced a powerful religious community become a helpless political minority. With the departure of the British, the Akali Dal leadership's hope of recreating a new Khalsa Raj collapsed and the period closed on a profoundly sad note: Hindus got Hindustan, Muslims got Pakistan, but what did the Sikhs get? The vivisection of "the Sikh land" was manifested when the Sikhs' formally appended an appeal to their daily prayer, seeking divine help for free access to sacred sites in the Western Punjab, which had now become part of the new country of Pakistan.

The dream of sovereignty

Partition gave rise to a new reality. As refugees from the west of the border settled down on the Indian side, the Sikhs found themselves with majority status in the central Punjab. Sikh leaders had known of the Jewish migration to Palestine, but they were not able to envision the type of demographic change that was to follow the partition of the Punjab. The new situation nursed hope for the future.

These developments provided considerable boost to Sikh religious life. The SGPC continued to serve as the custodian of Sikh interests and the maintainer of historic gurdwaras. The SGPC organized the Sikh History Research Board, and under its auspices scholars began to work on textual and historical subjects. The Sikh Reference Library and the Central Sikh Museum were built; the library housed a major collection of over a thousand early scriptural manuscripts and other related texts. In 1966, on the basis of a report prepared by Giani Gurdit Singh, the SGPC authorities formally elevated the Damdama Sahib, Talvandi Sabo, a site associated with Guru Gobind Singh, to the status of a Takhat. The effect of this addition was to raise the number of Takhats to five, a significant number in Sikh thinking, as well being a response to the aspirations of the Malwa Sikhs. The SGPC continued its interest in education and developed an extensive publication program. Its budget has expanded to cross the $4 million mark in 2003.

Local congregations continued to build new gurdwaras to meet their devotional needs, so that currently it is hardly conceivable that a Punjabi village or a town is without a gurdwara. The period also saw the centennial celebrations of Guru Gobind Singh's birth in 1966, Guru Nanak's birth in 1969, the martyrdom of Guru Tegh Bahadur in 1975, and the declaration of the Khalsa in 1999. New gurdwaras, museums, and colleges were built as part of these celebrations.

In addition, the establishment of the Punjabi University, Patiala, in 1962, and Guru Nanak Dev University, Amritsar, in 1970, have contributed considerably to the area of Sikh studies. Both of these universities have developed large departments of religious studies and Sikh history, and have worked hard to create a conducive environment and resources for serious scholarship in the field. J.S. Grewal, the leading scholar of this period, is recognized as the father of modern Sikh and Punjab studies.

While Sikh religious life has continued to thrive, Sikh leadership's political aspirations have resulted in a constant tug of war with the federal government. The battle lines were drawn immediately after the partition of the Punjab. Having once failed to avoid partition, the national leadership made "the unity and integrity" of the country its top priority and no challenge to it was to be permitted. Master Tara Singh (1885–1967), the preeminent Akali Dal leader, is on record as demanding as early as February 1948: "we want to have a province where we can safeguard our culture and tradition." He had already declared: "I want the right of self-determination for the Sikh Panth in matters religious, social and political." In taking this position, the Akali Dal's representatives abstained from signing the Indian constitution.

In 1951, the Akali Dal took up the issue of language, and demanded a state in which Punjabi would be the majority language. The national leadership rightly interpreted the demand as a cover for the establishment of a Sikh state and the local Hindus vehemently opposed this. The Akali Dal's efforts to work with the Congress failed miserably. After a prolonged struggle, which lasted until 1966, the Punjabi Suba was the last separate language state in India to come into being. For the Akali Dal, this arrangement was an interim one, as the ultimate goal was, of course, to establish a religious Sikh state. The new situation brought a strengthened Akali Dal together with a weakened Jan Sangh, the Hindu party that had opposed the demand of the Punjab Suba, this time united in a common goal to defeat the Congress.

Although Sikh leaders such as Swaran Singh and Manmohan Singh in Congress and Harkishan Singh Surjeet in the Communist Party have left a mark on the national scene, their impact on Punjab politics has been minimal. Giani Zail Singh (1917–94), the most prominent Congress Sikh leader in the Punjab, consistently used Sikh religious symbolism to consolidate his base of support. In the 1970s, as chief minister of the Punjab, he presented himself as the guardian of Sikh interests. The Akali Dal confirmed its position as representing Sikh aspiration by passing a formal resolution at Anandpur in 1973, which read: "As directed by Guru Gobind Singh and firmly etched on the pages of Sikh history and every Sikh heart, the goal of the Khalsa is political supremacy (*bol bala*)."

When Giani Zail Singh lost power in 1977, he continued to challenge the Akali Dal, and brought Sant Jarnail Singh Bhindranwale, head of a Sikh seminary in Mehta, into the limelight as their potential opponent. A purist who led devotional worship and inspired the Sikhs to undergo the *khaṇḍe di pahul*, Sant Bhindranwale, however, quickly outgrew his mentor's plans for him and emerged as a leader on the religio-political scene. A young charismatic figure thoroughly immersed in Sikh scriptural writings, history, and mythology, he shared the Akali Dal's ideological long-term agenda of Sikh sovereignty, but in his vision this was a Sikh right, not a gift from New Delhi. He disapproved of the "transactional" nature of the Akali Dal's activity, and was ready to fight, till death if necessary, to achieve these communal goals. By setting a personal example, he hoped to remind the Sikhs of their old tradition of martyrdom.

In July 1982, Sant Bhindranwale moved to the Darbar Sahib precincts and quickly absorbed its theo-political ethos. He would participate in the daily prayers at the Darbar Sahib and then hold his court on the roof of the *langar* building. For many Sikhs, their circumambulation of the Darbar Sahib would not be complete until they had gone to listen to him. The simplicity of his message touched a raw nerve in the community. Here was someone they could trust, someone who spoke the language they understood, above all, someone who did not ask anything for himself and who was willing to make the ultimate sacrifice of laying down his life to revive Sikh respect.

The most active support came from the Sikh Students' Federation (SSF), an organization started in the 1940s with its primary membership coming from Sikh institutions of higher learning in the Punjab. Sant Bhindranwale's message centered on the revival of Sikh nationalism with all the glory it entailed, and his willingness to initiate a battle for a separate state of Khalistan fired the young Sikhs' imagination. Other heterogeneous groups, such as retired Sikh army officers, civil servants, and intellectuals, joined him.

Sant Bhindranwale's radical position put the Akali Dal and national politics into disarray and left little space for many to maneuver their way around him. Those who challenged his point of view came under threat of elimination. The situation became explosive in June 1984, when the Indian army clamped the martial law in the Punjab, invading the Darbar Sahib and more than twenty other historic gurdwaras. It is not clear why the date selected for this move was the martyrdom day of Guru Arjan, when a large number of Sikhs had gathered to celebrate the event at these places. At the Darbar

The Akal Takhat after Operation Bluestar, 1984. Photograph.
Courtesy of Satpal Singh Danish, Amritsar, Punjab.

Sahib, the battle lasted three days, during which heavy artillery
was used to flush out the supporters of Sant Bhindranwale. When
"Operation Bluestar" came to a close, many had died, and the figures
range from 500 to 10,000, depending upon what sources one refers
to. The Akal Takhat was severely damaged (see above), and the
Sikh reference library with its rare collection was leveled into
ashes. The Sikhs were horrified to see the episode unfold. Many
suggested preserving the damaged building as a symbol of how far
"Hindu India" would go if the Sikhs lay claims for autonomy.

Indira Gandhi, the Indian prime minister at that time, defended
"Operation Bluestar," and invoked arguments of "national unity
and integrity." The Sikh response was different. Sikh soldiers in the
Indian army rebelled in several places and in one instance killed their
commanding officer. Two of Mrs. Gandhi's Sikh bodyguards assassi-
nated her on October 31, 1984. While not condoning such an act,
it is certain that she had underestimated the depth of pain her actions
had caused the Sikhs.

Sant Bhindranwale became more powerful after his death, since for many he came to symbolize Sikh political aspiration in all its purity. However, his legacy of violent struggle eventually reached a dead-end. The militant movement petered out for want of centralized leadership and an evolving ideology. Leaders came and went, but no-one could replace him. His flag-bearers failed to control the mindless violence of a purely criminal nature that engulfed the Punjab in the 1980s and eroded the very basis of their movement. Nor was there any successful ideological effort to delineate the specific contours of Khalistan.

In 1992, an election was held without the participation of the Akali Dal, and 24 per cent of people, largely from urban areas, voted. The Congress party received 44 per cent of the votes, with 11 per cent of the total population supporting him, Beant Singh was elected the chief minister. In the years that followed, K.P.S. Gill, the state police chief, literally wiped out all those who showed even the slightest sign of being sympathetic to the Khalistan movement. These atrocities, along with the rising corruption under Beant Singh's leadership, resulted in the Congress party's rout in 1997. The Akali Dal–Bharatiya Janata Party, the new name of the old Jan Sangh, returned to power with a large majority.

Prakash Singh Badal, the Akali Dal chief minister, was expected to work towards protecting Sikh interests while simultaneously building a broader cooperation between the Hindus and the Sikhs. During his tenure, Badal certainly worked his way successfully toward attaining supremacy in Sikh politics. He was the first leader in the last quarter of the century to control three centers of Sikh political power. He was the chief minister of the state, the president of the Akali Dal, and was able to place a person of his choice as the president of the SGPC.

But, as it turned out, Badal was unable to think beyond maintaining power and building a political dynasty. The ideology of Hindu–Sikh cooperation only served as an instrument of electoral politics to capture and then sustain power. No creative effort was made to address the issues confronting the Sikhs or the region in general. Badal's government was voted out in February 2002, and the Congress under the leadership of Amarinder Singh, a scion of the Patiala ruling family, won the reins of power for the next five years. In its first year, the new government's energy has been geared toward unveiling the corruption of its predecessor, and the direction of its own governance has yet to emerge. The Punjab is in the process of rising from the violence of the past decades.

Toward a world community

The developments of the last quarter of the nineteenth century resulted in considerable internal movement. For those who enlisted in the British army and police, the possibility of moving away from the Punjab became a fact of life. The migration of a hundred Sikhs to Hong Kong in 1867 was followed by the deployment of the Indian army in the Sudan and in the Mediterranean. With the construction of railroads in East Africa in the mid-1890s, the Sikhs arrived in large numbers there. By the beginning of the twentieth century, Sikhs had reached the western coast of North America. By 1920, they had built gurdwaras in Shanghai, Hong Kong, Malaya, Singapore, Burma, East Africa, London, Vancouver and Stockton, California.

During the past decades, the number of Sikhs who have left the Punjab has increased considerably. At present, around two million Sikhs live overseas, occupying a full range of occupational niches, from professional positions to non-skilled labor, and they have successfully constructed an elaborate network of gurdwaras and Sikh organizations to preserve their culture. In fact, the Sikh religion has appealed to some living in other countries; for example, a small group of people who were of Euro-American descent joined Sikhism in the 1970s under the religious guidance of Harbhajan Singh Yogi (b. 1929), a Punjabi Sikh who came to the United States in 1968.

To sum up, these three chapters have traced the challenges that confronted the Sikh community as well as its successes during the past five centuries. Presently, the community has a firm base in the Punjab, which is considered the Sikh homeland. In the heart of this region stands the Darbar Sahib, the most revered Sikh site, from which the sound of sacred verses emanates around the clock. Although the overwhelming majority of Sikhs live in the Punjab, others have fanned out to different parts of India and to foreign lands, including Australia, eastern Africa, western Europe, and North America. With Sikh flags flying in the gurdwaras built in these distant places, the community is entering the new millennium with a firm conviction of a bright future.

<table>
<tr><td>Beliefs and
Devotional Life</td><td>4</td></tr>
</table>

So far, Sikh beliefs have been mentioned in the context of their role in Sikh history. In this chapter, the focus is on what Sikh beliefs entail and the way they translate themselves into the daily lives of the Sikh community. After a brief introduction to the sources that serve as the basis for Sikh religious life, the second section examines the Sikh conception of the divine, the world, and the role of human beings within it. Finally, the third section looks at the way these beliefs have shaped the devotional and ceremonial life of the present-day Sikh community.

Sources

A wide variety of sources, ranging from the letters of the Gurus to nineteenth-century Sikh coins and medals, reveals a good deal about early Sikh beliefs and practice. Sikh guiding literature, however, remains perhaps the richest ground for details of the Sikh religion. This literature can be divided into two groups: the first is the Guru Granth, which enshrines the core revelation (M5, GG, 1226), enjoys a unique and uncontested status within the Sikh community, and serves as its primary source of beliefs and practice; the second group includes an array of writings which command varied authority and reverence, depending on when they were written and the figures associated with them. This second group can be further divided into three: the exegetical or interpretive literature based upon the Gurus' compositions and events of their lives; the poetry produced at Sikh courts at Ramdaspur and Anandpur; and the Rahit-related writings.

The Guru Granth
The history of the compilation of the Guru Granth is well documented.

It started with the creation of a volume of Guru Nanak's compositions at Kartarpur (in the 1530s). The contents of this text expanded in three stages: first, the Goindval Pothis (in the early 1570s), second, the Kartarpur Pothi (in 1604), and third, the Adi Granth (in the 1680s). The text of the Adi Granth was later elevated to the status of the Guru Granth, which is the Guru manifested in book form.

The text of the Guru Granth contains around three thousand poetic compositions created by six of the Gurus (Guru Hargobind, Guru Harirai, and Guru Harkishan did not write, and Guru Gobind Singh seemingly decided not to include his writings in this text), over a dozen bards at the sixteenth-century Sikh court, and fifteen non-Sikh saints. The ideas expressed in the compositions of the Gurus serve as the central point of reference and the other carefully selected writings conform to these ideas. Their authors came from a wide variety of social backgrounds, which added to the comprehensiveness of Sikh understanding of human experience.

The text opens with the symbol *Ek Oankar* (literally One Creator) (see symbol, below), which combines the first Gurmukhi numeral and letter and for Sikhs represents Vahiguru's unity. The text is divided into three parts. It has a liturgical section, comprising three daily prayers to be recited at sunrise, sunset, and at the end of the day. The main body contains thirty-one separate subsections organized according to a musical mode (*rag*) assigned for singing these verses. The final section includes miscellaneous compositions not set to music.

The text is carefully organized so that the compositions of Guru Nanak are positioned at the beginning, followed by those of his five successors, those of various Sikh bards, and finally those of the non-Sikh saints.

Ek Oankar. The text of the Japji is inscribed within it.
19th century. Courtesy of Guru Nanak Dev University, Amritsar, Punjab.

Because of the wide range of contributors, the language of Guru Granth shifts from the Punjabi of Shaikh Farid, a thirteenth-century Sufi poet, and that of the Gurus, to that of Sant Bhasha, a lingua franca used by the medieval saints of north India.

Manuscripts containing sacred verses were seen as the repository of revelation and were assigned authority from their very genesis. This paved the way for Guru Gobind Singh's elevation of the sacred text to the status of the Guru Granth, when he transferred to it the authority previously held by the personal Guru. The authority to interpret the text was assigned to the Guru Panth. In this role, the Guru Granth enjoys the central position in Sikh devotional life. The text is offered royal treatment with all the regalia of a court. It is covered in brocade, always placed under a canopy, and it is taken care of by an attendant who fans it with a ceremonial flywhisk. If it has to be moved from one place to another, it must have an appropriate retinue to follow it, and it is carried on the head, thus emphasizing its purity and sacredness. All supplications that formally close Sikh prayers

Sikh women in gurdwara at Stockton, California, 1927. Photograph. Courtesy of Sohan Singh Pooni, British Columbia, Canada.

are addressed to the text, which then is opened at random and the composition appearing at the left-hand top corner is considered to be the *hukam*, the divine reply to the appeal. When the text grows old, it is taken to Goindval and ceremonially cremated. (See page 74.)

The interpretive literature

Writings, both in poetry and prose, which explained and interpreted the teachings and the activities of the Gurus began to be created early in the tradition. Bhai Gurdas, the first prominent contributor to this literature, wrote thirty-nine ballads (*vars*, containing more than 800 stanzas), and over 650 short poems (*kabitts*). In his ballads, written in Punjabi, he narrates episodes from the lives of the Gurus and interprets their teachings for his fellow Sikhs. His short poems are in Braj, a language used in central India, and as a result are less known among Sikhs than his ballads.

The Janam Sakhis that developed during the seventeenth century fall in four lines: the Puratan, the Miharban, the Bala, and the Adi Sakhis. These stories communicate Guru Nanak's message as well as demonstrate the close relationship between his actions and his teachings. Though the focus of this literature remained on Guru Nanak, the genre expanded to include a large text about Guru Amardas, and episodes about other Gurus. The "martial deeds" and "majesty" of Guru Hargobind and Guru Gobind Singh created a variant form called the Gurbilas (splendor of the Guru). Sainapati was the first writer in this genre, and several others employed it in the eighteenth and nineteenth centuries. This literature continues to serve as a primary source of introduction to the Gurus' lives in Sikh religious settings.

Court poetry

Compositions in this genre began to be produced early in the Sikh tradition by bards such as Mardana, Satta and Balvand, Sundar, and the Bhatts, who served as resident poets at Ramdaspur. There is no access to their earlier writings, if there were any, but the compositions they created about the majesty of the Gurus and their courts are included in the Guru Granth. Indeed, Satta and Balvand's couplet:

> The radiance descends from the heavens,
>   where the Sovereign's praises are sung.

> Gazing at you, true Sovereign,
> the filth of the past lives is washed away (GG, 967)

has attained liturgical status since it is recited when the text of the Guru Granth is ceremonially opened.

The story of the literature produced at the court at Anandpur is, however, more complex. There are references to at least fifty-two resident poets and their actual number definitely exceeded that. A large body of the extant writings of this period gives the impression of being created for a broader audience but presented at the Sikh court. These largely deal with non-Sikh themes, and in two cases, there are efforts to update the existing compositions with a concluding segment that focuses on Sikh beliefs. These poets primarily wrote in Braj, but also used Persian, and Punjabi, and they employed a plethora of literary forms and meters in their poetry.

The literature of the Sikh court falls into three main categories. The better-known of these is a compilation that later came to be named the **Dasam Granth** (the tenth book or book of the tenth Guru). The second part includes texts such as the *Sarab Loh Granth* (book of all iron), the *Pothi Prem Ambodh* (book of poets of love), and so on, which claim to have been produced at Anandpur. The *Sarab Loh Granth* is a bulky text containing over 6,500 poetic stanzas, only thirty of which deal with the theme of the Khalsa and are known among the Sikhs. Finally, there are references in eighteenth-century sources to compilations such as the *Avtar Lila* (play of divine incarnations), the *Samund Sagar* (sea of seas), the *Vidaya Sagar* (sea of knowledge), all of which are no longer extant.

The Dasam Granth comprises three sections, the *Bachitar Natak* (the wondrous drama), the *Pakhayn Charitar* (the stories of women), and a set of miscellaneous compositions. In the *Bachitar Natak*, the poets sing of the divine incarnations of Vishnu, Shiva, Devi, and Hazrat Muhammad/Mehdi. The general impression that it would have conveyed to the Sikhs at Anandpur is that Guru Gobind Singh belonged to this illustrious line of incarnations and, in tune with his predecessors, was involved in eradicating evil from the world. The *Pakhayn Charitar* includes poetic compositions on a wide variety of secular themes containing characters such as monks from Tibet, Portuguese traders, and women of easy virtue. This portion has been difficult to reconcile with other Sikh values and its presence has been a source of tension in the tradition.

Among the remaining compositions in the Dasam Granth are found the *Jap* (meditation in 196 short verses), the *Savayye* (panegyrics in thirty-three verses), the *Chaupai* (a set of twenty-five rhyming verses), and a couplet, all of which are now part of Sikh liturgy. In addition, the *Apani Katha* (my own story in thirty-three verses), the *Chandi di Var* (the ballad of the goddess Chandi in fifty-five verses), nine short compositions set to music called *Shabad Hazare* (thousand words) containing twenty-seven verses, and the *Zafarnama* (the letter of victory containing 111 verses) play a limited role in Sikh worship. With the exception of these compositions, the remaining text recorded in 1,428 printed pages is basically unknown.

Regarding the history of its compilation, its attribution, and its role within the community, the Dasam Granth defies consensus. It is known that Guru Gobind Singh, if he was a contributor, did so without employing the authoritative signature of "Nanak." Kesar Singh Chhibbar, the only eighteenth-century writer who mentions the compilation of a "a junior Granth" at Anandpur, reports that Guru Gobind Singh declared its contents as "our pla,." not to be appended to the Guru Granth. Having said that, Chhibbar goes on to offer his own gloss on the situation and suggests that "let us treat both the texts [the Guru Granth and the other Granth] as the Guru and the smaller compilations as their children." Yet these remain his words.

The Dasam Granth has been and continues to be treated with respect in places associated with Guru Gobind Singh, such as Patna and Nander. The Nihangs (fearless), a small group of Sikhs, revere it, but it is important to note that they also attribute the *Sarab Loh Granth* to Guru Gobind Singh and accordingly treat it with great reverence. Though more research needs to be done on the history of its compilation and its role within the community, there is absolutely no evidence that the Dasam Granth ever competed with the Guru Granth's authority.

The Rahitnamas

As previously discussed, statements about Rahit appear in the compositions of the Gurus, in their letters of command (**hukamnamas**) sent to distant congregations, and in the form of short entries recorded on the opening folios of Sikh scriptural manuscripts. Bhai Gurdas and the Janam Sakhi literature provide additional details regarding Sikh beliefs and practice. During the early period, however, the activities of the Gurus served as the model for the Sikhs to emulate and if the question of what needed to be done ever arose, the Guru was there to provide the community with an authoritative answer.

Yet the declaration of the Khalsa created an unprecedented situation because, on the one hand, it required a more elaborate Rahit, and, on the other, it paved the way for phasing out the office of the Guru, and with it an authoritative figure to answer questions. The result was the creation of the Rahitnamas—manuals of Sikh belief and practice. There are references that show that the first text of this type was prepared in 1701. It has not survived but a version seems to have been incorporated in a text attributed to Chaupa Singh.

Chaupa Singh makes three observations regarding the nature of Rahit. First, he says, the Rahit is specifically addressed to "the Sikhs and no one else", thus it is not a universal code of beliefs and ethics but a set of rules to be followed only by the Sikhs. Second, there is one Rahit and all Sikhs share it (*sanjhi*). Finally, he states that the Rahit recorded by him is by no means comprehensive. If the Sikhs wanted to add something to its contents, they could do so as long as the addition was within the spirit of Sikh beliefs enshrined in the Guru Granth. The authority of the Rahit is rooted in the revelation but it is clearly understood as an evolving set of rules designed to meet the needs of the community in changing circumstances.

Sikh savants continued to write their versions of the Rahit in response to the needs of the time and some of these documents are extant. However, these remain personal statements that reflect on the needs of the Sikh community at various junctures in Sikh history. Toward the end of the nineteenth century, with the coming of the printing press, the need to generate a single authoritative document presenting the Rahit became clear. The process was a lengthy one, reaching its completion in the Rahit Maryada compiled under the auspices of the SGPC in 1950. Since then, this collectively created document has successfully served as the standard of Sikh belief and conduct.

Beliefs

The Sikhs call their beliefs gurmat, and they are constructed around two basic assumptions. First, the content was revealed to the Gurus and is thus of divine origin. Second, the search for and the knowledge of truth are important, but living with these aims is the paramount goal of Sikh life (M1, GG, 62). The gurmat thus constitutes both belief and practice. A belief that does not find expression in practical action has no place in Sikh thought (M1, GG, 903).

Vahiguru (God)

The Sikhs believe in the unity and unique nature of Vahiguru. They are fiercely opposed to any anthropomorphic conceptions of the divine. Hence Vahiguru has no relatives, no mother, no father, no wife, no son, no rival who may become a potential contender (M1, GG, 597). Vahiguru is omnipotent and omnipresent, the transcendent Sovereign who became immanent as the creation came into being (M1, GG, 1036, 1038). There is, however, a fundamental polarity between Vahiguru and the creation, which leaves no provision for divine incarnation. Vahiguru is essentially different from the world and consequently is beyond human language and categories such as gender.

Vahiguru runs the world with justice and grace. The principle of justice represents the stern aspect of divine nature: Vahiguru the father figure destroys evil and supports good (M1, GG, 1028), and in the process uses human beings as instruments in human history. Guru Nanak believed that Indian rulers who had become corrupt deserved moral retribution, which came in the form of the Mughal invasion (M1, GG, 360). Vahiguru bestows power and withdraws power from political rulers, and brings about changes in nature with oceans becoming dry land and mountains submerging under deep seas (M1, GG, 144).

In loving and gracious aspect, Vahiguru the mother figure listens to the prayers of human beings and fulfills their wishes. Vahiguru pardons their wrongdoings and continues to love and care for them. Divine grace is all-powerful and can wash away all previous evil. It can transform a heron (the symbol of hypocrisy) into a swan (purity) (M1, GG, 1171). Grace is by its very nature a divine gift, and it cannot be acquired as a matter of right. Nonetheless, human beings are expected to prepare themselves actively to receive it.

The clarity of Guru Nanak's conception of a non-incarnated personal Vahiguru as a just, loving, caring sovereign, who runs the world with the divine command, brings it closer to Semitic religious thought. The central metaphor used to envision Vahiguru is that of a sovereign, and epithets such as Sahib, Khasam, and Patishah, all from Arabic and Persian, traceable to the Torah via the Quran, appear with great frequency in Guru Nanak's writings.

Jagat (world)

Guru Nanak created a cosmology hymn in which brief answers to basic questions about the genesis of the universe are addressed (M1, GG, 1035–6).

> For endless eons, there was only darkness.
> Nothing except the hukam existed.
> No day or night, no moon or sun;
> Vahiguru alone sat in a primal stance. ...
> When Vahiguru so willed, creation came into being...
> Without any support Vahiguru erected the universe...
> The Unmanifested One revealed itself in the creation.

A single divine call resulted in the rise of complicated structures with the sky, the earth, and all the myriad of forms of vegetation and life (M1, GG, 3; M 5, GG, 1003). Although only Vahiguru knows the details, all this happened in historical time, that is, the creation of human beings is simultaneous with the creation of the world, and human history follows a divine design.

For the Sikhs, the universe by definition represents divine immanence. It cannot reach the purity of divine attributes, and is not true or eternal when compared to the reality of Vahiguru, but as the divine creation it enjoys a high level of truth and beauty (M1, GG, 463, 580). It is a lush green meadow, where the lives of human beings unfold (M1, GG, 142, 418, 843); Vahiguru is fully involved in the day-to-day running of the world (M1, GG, 1331), and is a farmer who prepares the field, sows the seed, and waits to see it bloom in human hearts (M1, GG, 19). The divine activity parallels that of a potter who shapes humans and other figures (M1, GG, 935), and enjoys watching the results of this activity in the world (M1, GG, 2).

Guru Nanak mentions Shiva, Vishnu, and Devi and their incarnations, but they are understood to be part of the creation, and therefore subject to the same predicament as human beings (M1, GG, 1153). The Hindu doctrine of Maya, which deludes human beings into accepting the empirical world as reality, Kala, the power that limits the universal condition of external existence, and Karma, an autonomous system of justice that is articulated through cause and effect, provide the context for conversation, but are summarily dismissed as subservient to the divine command and consequently powerless in the larger scheme of things.

Manas (human beings)

For Guru Nanak, human life is a precious jewel (M1, GG, 156) and its goal is to attain liberation, which is to be one with Vahiguru by having a respectful place in the divine court (M1, GG, 942). The search for liberation works at two distinct levels—the spiritual and the temporal—which are closely interwoven. The first level concerns a relationship with Vahiguru while the second concerns a relationship with fellow human beings, and the world in general.

Before we examine this, let us look at the Sikh concept of the Guru. For the Sikhs, the Guru is a special being, the bearer of the divine word (M1, GG, 466). He is like the sandalwood tree, which imparts fragrance to whoever comes near it (M1, GG, 990). He helps his followers destroy self-centeredness (M1, GG, 2 and 469) and attain liberation (M1, GG, 930, 942, 946). The Guru is also the overall leader of the community, responsible for its spiritual and temporal welfare. Service to the Guru is an important virtue (M1, GG, 635).

In more specific terms, Guru Nanak had a revelation and the reflection that emerged from that experience resulted in the founding of the Sikh community. His nominated successor by virtue of his elevation to this status also had a special relation with Vahiguru. As mentioned earlier, the relationship of the nine successor Gurus with each other and with Guru Nanak is understood through the doctrine of the unity of Guruship (Satta and Balvand, GG, 967), which includes the idea of Guru Granth as representing the living Guru.

According to Sikh belief, a spiritual journey begins with a clear recognition of the nature of Vahiguru and the world. Vahiguru is the only rightful object of human prayers (M1, GG, 1345), and the devotional experience is shaped by the feelings of awe (*bhai*) and love (*bhau*) of the divine majesty and grace (M1, GG, 465, 831). It is necessary to sing and listen to the divine praise and attempt to hold the divine presence in constant remembrance (M1, GG, 2). The real impediment is the human mind, which suffers from a fundamental flaw of self-centeredness (**haumai**), and as a result, human beings tend to see themselves as masters of their own destiny. This state of mind prevents them from recognizing their humble place in this universe created by Vahiguru. The mind is naturally fickle and tends to be attracted to and involved in material pursuits. For this reason, bringing the mind under control becomes a pre-requisite to effect spiritual elevation.

In addition, a person's activity in the world could help or hinder them on the path toward Vahiguru (M1, GG, 1330). The Rahit, which defines the norm of Sikh belief and conduct, works at individual, familial, communal, and social levels (M1, GG, 831, and 1343). At the personal level, this code involves the cultivation of values such as compassion, contentment, duty, effort, humility, purity, service, and the control of the instincts of anger, covetousness, greed, attachment to worldly goods, and pride (M1, GG, 503).

The image of the home recurs with great frequency in the writings of the Gurus. In their view, liberation is not achieved in isolation or renunciation, but within the context of family and domestic responsibility (M1, GG, 61). Thus, the cultivation of the individual self leads to a highly evolved ethic of familial responsibility. Guru Nanak also created a significant space for women to establish themselves as useful members of the community and society.

Family ethic is further expanded to include obligations toward the good of the community, which implies a life of high social commitment. Religious life demands the qualities of hard work, as well as the need to share the fruit of their labor with others (M1, GG, 1245), and commitment to service (M1, GG, 26). Though humility is a virtue, it must be dignified humility. A life without dignity is worse than death (M1, GG, 142, and 358), and it is important to command the respect of others (M1, GG, 1127, 1188). Guru Nanak's ideal human being is a productive and well-respected member of the community.

Ultimately, Guru Nanak believed that human beings are required to relate to society at large as well as to the natural world around them. As part of the divine creation, all people—irrespective of their color and features—are related, and should have respect for each other and sensitivity toward the natural world. Building on this belief, his successors would run *langars*, dig wells to supply water, and supplicate for the welfare of all (M3, GG, 1358; M5, GG, 533, 815, 1357, 1358). The need to show kindness toward all people as well as the natural world (*parupkar*) would shape Sikh views on socio-political-ecological ethics.

Guru Nanak uses the metaphor of monarchy to alert the rulers to their responsibility of meting out justice and taking care of the weak and the helpless. If authorities continue to perpetuate injustice, this oppression is to be actively resisted. The earlier Gurus' belief in fearlessness and the professed need to live a life of dignity culminated in Guru Gobind Singh's declaration of the community as the Khalsa and the establishment of the Khalsa Raj as its goal. This was seen to be the only appropriate setting in which the special relationship between the Sikhs and their Creator could be developed.

The poets at Anandpur sang of reciting the name of Vahiguru while preparing for a holy war (***dharmyudh***). For Guru Gobind Singh, when routine means of obtaining justice fail, physical force is fully justified. The ethic of the war that was to be waged was based on Guru Nanak's belief that a bloody fight between armies was a fair contest, but that the harassment of ordinary people was not acceptable (M1, GG, 360). As far as the Sikhs were concerned, death that came while fighting for the right cause would lead them straight to liberation (M1, GG, 580). Becoming a martyr was another model for mystical ascension. However, while fighting, the Sikhs of the Gurus were not permitted to scar the landscape by burning crops and villages alike, a common Afghan practice of the time.

Devotional activity

In Sikh devotions, men, women, and children submit themselves to Vahiguru (M1, GG, 474), sing and listen to the divine praises (M1, GG, 2), give thanks for the gift of human birth and the bounties that accompany it (M1, GG, 414), and seek help with the problems that may confront them (M5, GG, 519). The experience of prayer is both personal and congregational, though the Sikhs firmly believe that the collective supplication of a congregation never goes unfulfilled. Prayer could be held at any time and anywhere, because it is the recitation of the divine word that makes the time and the spot auspicious (M5, GG, 562, 816). Sikh sacred compositions are largely set to music, but the use of music serves as an instrument for the esthetic enjoyment of the participants and is not essential to devotions as such (M4, GG, 1423).

Worship

The Guru Granth constitutes the center of both personal and congregational Sikh worship, and Sikh devotions typically include scriptural recitation (*paṭh*), the singing of the sacred verse with musical accompaniment, and listening to their elucidation. Reflection on the sacred verses and listening to a commentary on them is essential as it enables the participants to understand the content of Sikh teachings and to translate these ideas into their daily activities (M3, GG, 594). Service (*seva*) is also considered part of the worship. These traditions can be traced back to the inception of the community.

The Sikhs have three obligatory prayers to be performed daily. The sunrise prayer includes the recitation of Guru Nanak's *Japji* (meditation), and the *Jap* and the *Savayye*, both from the Dasam Granth. The sunset prayer contains the *Rahiras* (supplication), which includes nine compositions (four of Guru Nanak, three of Guru Ramdas, and two of Guru Arjan), five stanzas of the *Anand* of Guru Amardas, two couplets of Guru Arjan, all from the Guru Granth, and the *Chaupai*, a panegyric, and a couplet, from the Dasam Granth. The *Sohila* (praise), the last prayer of the day recited just before going to sleep, includes five compositions (three of Guru Nanak, one of Guru Ramdas, and one of Guru Arjan). Many devoted Sikhs also recite Guru Nanak's ballad in Asa *rag*, in the morning, and Guru Arjan's *Sukhmani* (jewel of peace), during the day.

A reading of the entire Guru Granth is considered a highly pious activity. Family members, both male and female, often undertake this reading over a period lasting from six months to one year. A reading of the text completed in a week and an unbroken reading (*akhan,ḍo paṭh*) taking forty-eight hours, mark special occasions such as moving into a new house or marriage. In the latter readings, the help of family, friends, or professional readers in the nearby gurdwara is sought. These readings also take place in gurdwaras.

Congregational worship is considered to be attending a "court" (*divan*), with the text of the Guru Granth, the sovereign of the Sikhs, adorning the throne. As previously mentioned, all the symbols of royalty, such as a canopy, a ceremonial flywhisk, and an attendant are present. As a mark of respect, men, women, and children have their heads covered, submit themselves to the presence of the divine word by touching their foreheads to the ground in front of the text, then sit and participate in the congregational singing, the supplication, and finally listen to the *hukam*. The prayers are followed by the distribution of the *karah prashad*, blessed food prepared with equal quantities of sugar, flour, and clarified butter. The *karah* came from Punjabi culture, where it serves as a marker of celebration. After its distribution, the congregation discusses any day-to-day problems. Social and political issues are regarded as related to religious activity and speakers are available to report about challenges confronting the community. What is discussed at these gatherings is a fair indicator of concerns and tensions within the community at that time.

The service closes with the *langar*, during which the participants share food. All sit and eat without any age, caste, gender, or status distinctions. The seventeenth-century traditions report that meat was served at the *langar*, but as a mark of respect for those who do not eat meat, the food offered there is now always vegetarian. The *langar* provides a way of expressing gratitude for the divine bounty by sharing its fruit with others; it offers the opportunity for service when helping to cook the food, serve it, and clean up; and it manifests Sikh solidarity and equality in the form of collective commensalism.

New technology has also had an affect on devotional practices. Loudspeakers at the gurdwara can bring the singing of sacred verses into neighbouring Sikh homes in the Punjab. Recorded cassettes of sacred music are now available and many Sikhs listen to them while traveling or while doing chores at home and at work. At present, the morning and evening prayers at the Darbar Sahib are broadcast on television and Sikhs in the Punjab can watch them while carrying on with their other activities. The daily *hukam* from the Darbar Sahib is available over the internet and many Sikhs all over the world start their day by reading that.

Ceremonies

Sikh ceremonies begin at birth and continue through to the very end of a person's life. Until recently, when children were born at home, a senior member of the family would put a drop of honey in the baby's mouth while reciting the invocation used in the Guru Granth (**mangal/mulmantar**) in the ear. This is called *gurati*. Soon after the birth, the family visits the gurdwara to offer supplication for a happy and healthy life for the baby, and to take the *hukam* from the text. The opening letter of the verse is used as the first letter in the name of the child. To this "Singh" for a male and "**Kaur**" for a female are added.

Some Sikhs append their family name to this. For instance, the three segments of Gurinder Singh Mann contain the first name, the marker of a male, and the family name.

Some young Sikhs, both male and female, undergo the *khaṇḍe di pahul* early in their adulthood. Undergoing this ceremony by a Sikh implies that he or she is willing to make a special commitment, which in a contemporary context means following the Rahit in the strictest possible way. They are not allowed to miss prayers, or part with the five ks. The *khaṇḍe di pahul* is thus a confirmation of a Sikh's commitment to his or her personal beliefs and to the community's welfare.

The settlement of a Sikh marriage continues to be a family affair, though the situation is changing with more young Sikh men and women taking the responsibility of finding a partner into their own hands. Preparations for the marriage ceremony often begin with a reading of the Guru Granth at the bride's home. During the ceremony itself, the bride and groom walk around the text of the Guru Granth four times while Guru Ramdas's *Lavan* is recited. The ceremony concludes with the congregation seeking divine blessings on the new couple's married life.

After death, the corpse is bathed and dressed in new clothes and placed on a pyre. The eldest son usually lights the pyre. The *Sohila* is recited while the pyre burns and a prayer is said to bring the ceremony to a close. The ashes are disposed of in a nearby stream or canal, and the bones are taken to Kiratpur, and thrown into the river Satluj at the spot where, according to Sikh traditions, Guru Hargobind's remains were dispersed. A reading of the Guru Granth is completed on the tenth, or some convenient, day when all relatives and friends can gather and collectively pray for the peace of the departed soul.

Festivals

The Sikhs follow the lunar calendar and perform special prayers twice a month. On the first day of each month, *sangrand*, Guru Arjan's *Baramah* (twelve months), is recited and supplication made for a happy month to follow. On the darkest night of the month, *masaya*, many Sikhs visit the Darbar Sahib, or a nearby gurdwara with a pool, and have a holy bath to purify the body before participating in the prayers. Early in their history, the Sikhs appropriated the local

Hindu festivals of Vaisakhi (spring), Divali (fall), and Holi (end of winter), and they continue to celebrate them. Over time, Sikhs have developed their own associations with these festivals. The Vaisakhi served as the day for the declaration of the Khalsa at Anandpur, so many Sikhs make a pilgrimage there to celebrate it. The Hola Mahala, or Sikh version of Holi, also attracts many Sikhs to Anandpur, the place of the festival's origin. The Darbar Sahib serves as the center for all Sikh celebrations. Those who cannot make a pilgrimage to Amritsar or Anandpur attend these celebrations at their local gurdwaras.

The other prominent dates in the Sikh calendar include the days associated with the lives of the Gurus (*gurpurab*). The birthdays of Guru Nanak and Guru Gobind Singh, and the martyrdom days of Guru Arjan and Guru Tegh Bahadur are given special attention. They are elaborately celebrated in the Darbar Sahib and the local gurdwaras. Some Sikhs make a pilgrimage to Nankana, the birthplace of Guru Nanak, and Patna, the birthplace of Guru Gobind Singh, to celebrate these anniversaries.

Sacred space

Although the Sikhs believe that the whole world is sacred since it is a divine creation, the *dharmsal* (place of worship) marked the sacred space in the early Sikh community. The congregational singing of the divine word sanctified the place. The gurdwara, the house of the Guru, served as the focus of Sikh sacred geography: here the recipient of the revelation himself led the religious singing. In the early period, there was one Guru and hence one gurdwara (his house), but after the dissolution of the office of the personal Guru, all *dharmsals* became gurdwaras, as the text of the Guru Granth was housed there. With the Guru Granth placed on a raised podium, a large room where congregational prayers can be held thus serves as a gurdwara. Its other two indicators include a Nishan Sahib, a saffron flag, which symbolizes the sovereignty of the place, and a *langar*, which provides a means for service and philanthropy.

Gurdwara

Chaupa Singh mentions four benefits that the Sikhs gain from a visit to the gurdwara. First, it provides them with the opportunity to listen to the word of the Guru and helps them to understand who they are. Secondly, they can listen to the Rahit and learn what they should or should not do. Third, they meet fellow Sikhs and get to know them. Finally, the visit would provide an opportunity for charity. Rahit literature reiterates that the Sikhs should always carry something in cash or kind with them to offer toward the community's welfare.

For Chaupa Singh, the gurdwaras fell into two categories. The first comprised those that were primarily built to serve as centers of religious worship, and the second included the historic gurdwaras associated with the ten Gurus and the Guru Granth, and the sites where Sikh blood was spilled fighting for a communal cause (Shahidganj). Sikh sacred space thus formally expanded to include the spots where the divine word was sung as well as the sites where Sikh historical events had unfolded.

In the first category, the simplest version of the gurdwara can be set up in the home. Usually, families use a spare room and place the Guru Granth there. The text is ceremonially opened (*prakash*) in the morning and put to rest after sunset (*sukhasan*). The women in the family invariably assume responsibility for the care of the text and the rest of the family gathers there at the time of prayers. The second version would include when a congregation from a particular residential neighborhood builds its own gurdwara. Since it serves the needs of a group of people, the gurdwara will have a **granthi**, literally the keeper of the Guru Granth, but in actual terms this is the caretaker of the gurdwara. In addition to the daily worship, ceremonies such as weddings are held at the gurdwara.

The Darbar Sahib

The historic gurdwaras serve as the markers of the divine design for the Sikhs and in this status are its pilgrimage centers. The Darbar Sahib is the most important with the five Takhats next in line. Its precincts had the honor of association with Guru Ramdas, Guru Arjan, and Guru Hargobind, and also became the battlefield for fights between Sikhs, and Mughals and Afghans who wanted to destroy the building. Many Sikhs place the sacking of the Akal Takhat building in 1984 as another episode in the long history of this most sacred and most embattled focus of worship.

Rebuilt on its original foundation in the 1760s, the architecture of the Darbar Sahib blends Islamic and Rajput elements and manifests Sikh beliefs in complex ways. Constructed in the middle of "the pool of nectar," the majestic building represents Sikh religiosity as described in the metaphors of a "duck" and a "lotus," both of which float on the surface of water without being affected by it (M1, GG, 938; M5, GG, 272), and also of a well-built raft, created to move the devotees across the world (M1, GG, 729). Dedicated to the Sovereign of sovereigns (Patshah-i-patshahan), the building holds the divine word, the Guru Granth. Devotees purify themselves with a dip in the pool, present themselves at the court with the Guru Granth in the seat of authority, and listen to the recitation and singing of its contents around the clock.

The Akal Takhat, the seat of Sikh temporal power, stands close by. Its building is constructed in such a way that it can serve as a security post to protect the gateway to the Darbar Sahib. The arms of the Gurus and those of the Sikhs who died fighting for the community adorn the Akal Takhat's center. As the instruments for obtaining temporal power, these arms are assigned a distinct place as well as ritual reverence. They are ceremonially put up for display in the morning and put to rest in the evening. As part of the ceremony, each of these items is formally introduced, by stating who owned it, and when it was used. The typical devotional activity at the Akal Takhat includes the singing of heroic songs (*vars*) composed around events and individuals in Sikh history and the regular administring of the *khande di pahul*. Daily prayers at the Akal Takhat conclude with the beating of a drum symbolizing the sovereignty of the community. The custodian of the Akal Takhat is assigned the title of the Jathedar, "the commander of a military detachment," and enjoys a considerable place of respect within the community.

All Sikhs circumambulate the complex by keeping the Darbar Sahib toward their right (clockwise). As they head toward it, the building of the Akal Takhat stands on the side, but as they come out the Akal Takhat confronts them. The sequence is profoundly significant—the religious needs lie at the center and come before other concerns. Furthermore, while participating in the prayers at the Darbar Sahib, the Akal Takhat is not visible, but as the leaders sit on the podium of the Akal Takhat, the Darbar Sahib is in full view, representing how religious beliefs shape decisions regarding temporal matters, not vice versa. After a visit to the Darbar Sahib and the Akal Takhat, devotees share the *langar*.

Above: The sarbat khalsa *approving the need for Khalistan, 1986. Photograph, courtesy of Satpal Singh Danish, Amritsar, Punjab. Below: Devotees waiting for food to be served at the langar of the Darbar Sahib, 2003.**

Land of the Punjab

The Darbar Sahib precinct is framed in an even larger context of sacred space. While Bhai Gurdas has sung of the spread of the Guru Nanak's praise in the "Punjab," the Janam Sakhi narrators welcome him back to "the land of Punjab" after his travels away from it. Although not articulated in precise terms, the descriptions leave little doubt that this was the holy land, which had the honor of serving as a cradle for the founder of the Sikh community. As history unfolded, the land of Guru Nanak's birth and Guru Gobind Singh's vision of the Khalsa Raj combined in the minds of their followers, resulting in the eighteenth-century myth of the land of the Punjab as a divine gift to the Sikhs. The ideology of Sikh sovereignty territorially based in the central Punjab has subsequently remained entrenched in the Sikh psyche. (See page 90.)

Over the centuries, the Sikh community has developed a comprehensive system of beliefs and practice. The Guru Granth serves as the repository of Sikh beliefs as well as the central point of reference in Sikh devotional life. Stories from the lives of the Gurus and the Rahit provide further structure to Sikh life. As the locus of Sikh faith, the Darbar Sahib emanates the divine word, and attracts

Sikh leaders sitting in the sarbat khalsa, *1986. Photograph. Courtesy of Satpal Singh Danish, Amritsar, Punjab.*

Sikhs from all over the world in pilgrimage. During the past three centuries, the Sikh community has gathered at the Akal Takhat, when and if the need arose, and decided the course of its destiny. With the inspiration of the Gurus, Guru Granth, and Vahiguru guiding their actions, Sikhs have weathered many storms and have successfully achieved a full membership for themselves among other religious communities of the world.

This chapter opens with a discussion of the structure of Sikh society; its internal divisions based on social background, religious observances, and varied understanding of the nature of religious authority. The second section addresses gender-related issues and traces the status of women during the past five centuries. The final section states the challenges confronting Sikhs as they change from a regional group into a world community. In so doing, there will be an opportunity to understand the intricacies of Sikh socio-religious life, both in the Punjab and in countries the Sikhs adopted during the twentieth century.

Structure of Sikh society

Guru Nanak believed that Vahiguru was the creator and protector of all human beings, and consequently they are entitled to live a life of respect and aspire to attain liberation (M1, GG, 83, 142). His successors fully endorsed this view with the result that Sikh religious life makes no allowance for hierarchical distinctions. All Sikhs irrespective of age, gender, or social status visit the gurdwara, take a bath in the same pool, participate in congregational prayers, partake of *karah prashad*, and later share *langar*. All those who undergo the ceremony of the *khande di pahul* take the nectar from the same bowl without assigning any significance to the social background of those who administer it. These practices have continued since the community's inception.

Does this imply that Sikh society is devoid of social differentiation? The answer, of course, is no. Like all religious communities, the Sikh community is comprised of diverse groups. The Sikh population has been historically concentrated in three geographical areas in the Punjab—the Majha, the Doaba, and the Malwa—and Sikhs living in these regions remained socially isolated from each other in their early history. During the twentieth century, however, increases in population movement and changes in the demography of the Punjab have increased social interaction between these regional groups, considerably reducing their geographic differences.

The diversity within Sikh society can be safely examined along vertical lines, which emerge from the distinctive past of those who embraced the Sikh beliefs; horizontal lines, which denote primarily the degree of religious observances or orthodoxy; and the divisions between the mainstream community that rejects personal authority in religious matters and other groups that trust the authority of a saintly figure and follow his version of Sikh teachings.

Vertical (social) divisions

Written in the late eighteenth century, *Sikhan di Bhagatmala* refers to Sikh society as comprised of two segments: the urban Sikhs who worked with "the hand-operated weighing scale (*takari*)," and others who lived in villages and worked on the land with "the plough (*hal*)." These two broadly defined groups possess diverse social compositions and have distinct histories. The 1881 Punjab census, the first to record various groups within the Sikh community in detail, helps us to understand the complexity of Sikh society.

The urban segment of the community has historically included those who had originally come from upper-caste Hindu background. Their numbers have remained very small. In 1881, they comprised around 6 per cent of the total Sikh population. The overwhelming majority of this segment came from among the Aroras and Khatris, two Punjabi trading castes, and the remaining came from among other high-caste Hindu groups, such as Brahmans. The history of their association with the Sikh community goes back to its very inception.

The urban Sikhs were also the first to move out of the Punjab, carrying their beliefs with them as they settled down in places on the trade route from Bukhara in central Asia to Dacca in the far east of India, and towns on the east and west coasts of India. Beginning with Bhai Gurdas and Chaupa Singh, many of them have distinguished themselves as scholars. Banda Singh was the first outstanding military leader to have emerged from this group.

The rural segment of Sikh society is divided into two distinct sections. The Jats, who constitute over two-thirds of the Sikh population, have traditionally been landowning farmers. They come from a nomadic background, started settled agriculture in the Punjab around the fifteenth century, and were the primary inhabitants of the area around Kartarpur. Guru Nanak's message, which centered on a life of self-respect, the ethics of hard work and charity, and the images of Vahiguru as a farmer would have appealed to these nomads-turned-farmers. The developing network of *manjis* in the sixteenth century indicates the quick spread of Sikh teachings in the rural areas of central Punjab. *Dabistan-i-Mazahib* reports that a large number of Jats served as Masands in the early seventeenth century

During the eighteenth century, the Jats played a dominant role in the establishment of the Khalsa Raj and formally elevated themselves to the status of nobility in the region. Since the arrival of the British in 1849, the Jats have served with a great sense of pride in the police and the army. They have also proved to be outstanding farmers, and since the 1960s have been responsible for converting the Punjab into the granary of the subcontinent. Baba Budha (d. 1631) was the first prominent community leader to emerge from this group and Sainapati was the first outstanding writer. Partly on account of their large numbers, the leadership of the Sikh community after the Guru period has largely stayed in Jat hands.

The second section of the rural Sikh society, which constitutes over 25 per cent of Sikh population, comprises those who provided ancillary services to the Jats. They had originally emerged from the lower end of the Hindu caste hierarchy and included the Chamars (leather workers), the Chhimbas (tailors, who worked for both the landowners and the other groups), the Chuhras (sweepers, who performed their traditional work throughout the year but worked as agricultural labor during the harvest season), the Jhinvars (water carriers), the Lohars (blacksmiths), the Nais (barbers, since the Sikhs did not cut their hair, their responsibilities shifted to arranging marriages and serving as messengers), and the Ramgarias (carpenters).

While carrying on their traditional responsibilities, they worked closely with the Jats and made significant contributions in the Sikh struggle for political sovereignty. From Bir Singh, who came from a Chuhra background and was one of the top five Sikh leaders in the

1730s, onward many Sikhs from this group have occupied positions of leadership. Koer Singh, for example, wrote an influential biography of Guru Gobind Singh in 1751, and later Dit Singh, a Sikh from a Chamar background, played the central role in the late nineteenth-century formulation of Sikh religious norms. The two past presidents of the SGPC and many others who serve as the custodians of the gurdwaras come from this section of Sikh society. The Ramgarias as a group have been singularly successful in the area of Sikh art.

The continued existence of these groups was seen to contradict the concept of Sikh ideal society, and writers, beginning with Sarup Singh Koushish in 1790, repeatedly evoke Guru Gobind Singh's command that the socio-religious past should not be replicated and that there was no justification for distinctions (*bhed*) within Sikh society. The late nineteenth-century Sikh leadership was acutely aware of the gap between Sikh religious norms and social realities and it made concerted efforts to bridge it. For a complex set of reasons, however, these distinctions have continued to survive.

The received wisdom creates the impression that the divisions within Sikh society are part of the legacy of the Hindu caste system from which the Sikh community had emerged. Yet this perception needs several qualifications. First, Sikh doctrine does not allow a system or an ideology of social stratification and the social realities thus are not accordance with Sikh beliefs. Second, unlike Hindu society, the Sikhs do not observe an accepted hierarchy; each of the Sikh groups mentioned above vies for positions of leadership. Third, rural Sikh society came from a low-caste background, making it unlikely that these peoples would propagate a system that had abused them. Finally, the Jats, who comprise over 66 per cent of the Sikh community, emerged from a pastoral background, had no access to Hindu rituals, and probably had very restricted social interaction with the settled community and its caste hierarchy.

In order to understand the continuation of social groups within Sikh society, the focus needs to rest on the internal dynamics of the Sikh community itself. Because the Jats comprise over 66 per cent of the community and constitute the largest single component, other groups are relegated to the status of small minorities. For instance, the Ramgarias, the second largest group within the Sikh community, constitute less than 7 per cent, the Chamars around 6 per cent, and all others less than 3 per cent of the total population.

Consequently, these smaller groups have felt the need to maintain their group cohesion and continued it thorough matrimonial alliances within their own groups.

The urban Sikhs have historically been in an unenviable situation. While they consider themselves to be the spiritual and the intellectual elite of the community—after all, all the Gurus had come from this group—their small numbers within the community have not permitted an adequate sense of security. In the post-Guru period, their caste-based, status-oriented leanings did not arouse much sympathy within a community dominated by the Jaṭs and others, whose imagination was fired by the establishment of the Khalsa Raj. Writing in 1769, Kesar Singh Chhibbar, a fourth-generation Sikh from a Brahman background, argued for special status for those who had joined the Sikhs from upper-caste Hindu backgrounds, but no one paid any attention to his appeal.

The urban Sikhs' concerns about their status within the Sikh community may have also resulted in slowing down the process of disengagement from their parent communities. Some among these Sikhs felt comfortable in maintaining social and marital ties with the large surrounding Hindu caste groups of their origin. This created further difficulties for them as well as the Sikh community at large. Among the urban Sikhs, even to the present day, if one of the males were to cut his hair, it would be understood that he had reverted to the Hindu fold. To circumvent this problem of having constantly to prove their religious identity, the urban Sikhs have increasingly tended toward orthodoxy and ritualism.

Furthermore, the relationship between some urban Sikhs and Hindus was often described in Punjabi metaphors of inseparability, such as that of the "contact between nails and the flesh" (*nahun mas da rishta*) and "sharing of food and marrying each other's daughters" (*roti beti di sanjh*). Scholars have often mistakenly regarded the closeness between some urban Sikhs and Hindus as typical of Sikh–Hindu relations. This supposed closeness, however, does not apply to over 90 per cent of the Sikhs, who have historically left their social antecedents behind and among whom the issue of marriage across religious traditions is non-existent.

Within the rural segment of the Sikh community, a different set of developments unfolded. Sikh doctrine of social equality and the egalitarian Jaṭ ethos helped to elevate the status of the Sikhs who had come from a low-caste background, and exceptional individuals, such as Jassa Singh Ahluwalia (1718–83) and Jassa Singh Ramgaria (1723–1803), attained positions of top leadership. Yet the existing Jajmani system, a network of mutual interdependence, did not allow people from this group to acquire land and consequently acquire upward social mobility. Writing in 1841, Rattan Singh Bhangu emphasized Guru Gobind Singh's elevation of the service-group Sikhs to the very top, but he was well aware that the Sikh community's success on this issue was limited.

The Sikh leadership's efforts to remove social distinctions within Sikh society confronted a unique situation in the mid-twentieth century. After independence, the Indian government extended an elaborate package of benefits to those who were thought to have suffered under caste discrimination in the past. Sikh leaders were well aware that there was no place for caste distinctions in Sikh doctrine and the groups within Sikh society were not castes along the Hindu model. Yet it feared that the rural Sikhs, who originally came from a low-caste background, might join the Hindu community in order to receive the privileges offered. Political expediency prevailed and the Sikh leadership decided to declare the rural Sikhs to be part of the low castes to help them obtain benefits. This further muddled the situation for the Sikh community as a whole and confirmed the Hindu leaders' view that the Sikhs were part of the larger Hindu fold.

At the start of the twenty-first century, several conflicting forces are at work. First, the traditional professions within Sikh society are undergoing changes with the Jats entering trade and service groups and moving into white-collar jobs. Such developments will impact on these groups' attitude toward each other. The movement of the Sikhs away from the Punjab has created an unprecedented situation, in which there is little justification for the survival of social distinction. After all a Jat and a Ramgaria working in identical jobs in a factory owned by a third party cannot sustain traditional rivalries. Sikh children born in their parents' adopted countries find it difficult to synchronize doctrinal assertions of social equality with their parents' expectation that they marry within their own social groups. Furthermore, the entry of Europeans and Americans to the Sikh fold suggests that you can be a Sikh without having to worry about social distinctions of the past.

Yet group consciousness has been useful to leaders, both religious and political, in creating a constituency of followers in the Punjab and elsewhere. The Ramgaria and Chamar leaders, for instance, have used this platform in England with a considerable degree of success. These groups have even built separate gurdwaras that serve as their center of power. At present, the situation seems fluid and it is difficult to predict whether Sikh society in time will maintain the status quo or attempt to close the gap between Sikh doctrine and practice by working toward the ideal of a society free of distinctions (*bharam bhed to bagair*).

Horizontal (religious) divisions

These divisions are simpler and define the degree of commitment to religious observance. In the writings of Guru Nanak, the community seems to fall in two groups: the ideal Sikhs, whom he calls Gurmukh, literally, those who look toward the Guru and follow the Rahit propounded by him, and the Manmukh, those who are focused on their own minds, and may claim that they follow the Rahit but actually do not (M1, GG, 831). Elaborations of these two segments of the early Sikh community appear in the writings of the later Gurus and Bhai Gurdas.

After Guru Gobind Singh's elevation of the community to the Khalsa, the points of reference underwent further expansion. For Chaupa Singh, the Khalsa comprised two segments: the first included the Kesdharis or Singhs, who had undergone the ceremony of the *khande di pahul* and had taken up the mission of establishing the Khalsa Raj. They represented the ideal Sikh emanating divine light (*didari*). The other group comprised the **Sahijdharis** (slow adopters), who did not undergo the *khande di pahul*. They were called half-ripe (*kache pile*) as if on their way to maturation.

By the mid-eighteenth century, however, the boundaries between these two groups began to blur. With Sikh political success, a large number of them began to keep their hair long and append Singh to their names without having undergone the *khande di pahul*. Given the late nineteenth-century need for precision, this blurring was removed by using three descriptive titles: the **Amritdharis** (the bearers of the *amrit* or nectar), the **Kesdharis** (the bearers of long *kes* or hair), and the **Sahijdharis** (the bearers of slowness). These groups continue to this day.

Among the Amritdharis, for example, the Nihangs, a small but colorful minority, trace their origin to the army of Guru Gobind Singh and continue to follow the tradition of martial arts, reverence of weapons, and distinct attire. The Nihangs are family people but live in colonies of their own, and only recently have they begun to open up to modernity, replacing their horses with other means of transportation. Other Amritdhari men and women, which make up a much larger group, carry on their daily life, be it farming, business, or service, while following the Rahit in its entirety.

The Kesdharis constitute the overwhelming majority within the Sikh community and form its backbone. These men and women are not easily distinguishable from the Amritdharis as all keep their hair uncut. The Kesdharis participate fully in Sikh religious life, and in their observance a wide variety of practice is reflected. Some may come close to the Amritdharis, with the exception of not having undergone the *khaṇḍe di pahul*, while others may be more easygoing, accepting that cutting hair is against the Sikh norm, but still trimming their hair and beards.

From among the Kesdharis a new group has recently emerged, which is comprised of those who initially grew up with long hair but at some point decided to cut it. Their reasons for doing so range from the need to conform to society at large, particularly if they live outside the Punjab, to a genuine discomfort about treating long hair as a religious symbol. They do, however, continue to use Singh or Kaur in their names and follow the Rahit as far as they can. An acceptable term to describe this group is yet to be coined.

The numbers of Sahijdharis may have been larger in the Punjab during the eighteenth century, but over time some of them have joined the Kesdharis, while others have returned to the Hindu fold. As a group they have only survived in Sindh, in present-day Pakistan, where some still live, while others have moved to different parts of the world. In addition to the Guru Granth, these Sahijdharis use Hindu sacred texts and are devoted to Muslim patron saints. In other words, they adhere to a much larger devotional framework, of which Sikh beliefs constitute one component. During the political crisis of the 1980s, their relationship with the mainstream Sikh community came under considerable stress, resulting in their withdrawal from the gurdwaras. With the change in the Punjab situation, however, they seem to be slowly reviving their earlier practices. Their presence raises the

61, 989, 1030), which further assigns a position of considerable importance to women as the guarantors of a peaceful, well-organized household.

Guru Nanak's successors continued in his belief in the importance of the family and home in the human pursuit for liberation. Guru Amardas denounced the custom of widow burning (M3, GG, 787), and there is evidence that he disapproved of the Islamic belief that women should wear the veil in public. Sikh men and women were expected to participate in congregational activity without any gender distinction. Guru Ramdas defined dowry as divine remembrance and not a burden for parents, which results in the unwelcome birth of daughters (M4, GG, 79), and Bhai Gurdas emphasized the merit of monogamy.

From the eighteenth century, the Rahit literature stressed women's full participation in religious life. They were expected to be the best-informed member of the household and able to instruct their husbands and children in matters of belief and practice. By the early nineteenth century, women began to take the *khande di pahul*, which does not seem to have been available to them previously. Female infanticide was barred and widow remarriages were encouraged. Respect for women is also reflected in repeated edicts against visiting prostitutes, mistreating the women of one's enemies defeated in battle, and against having interaction with those who "kill their daughters." Late nineteenth-century Sikh leadership continued to build on this and attempted to close the gaps between Sikh ideas and practices. The Rahit Maryada is emphatic that no distinction is to be made on the basis of gender as far as the following of the Rahit is concerned.

In a seventeenth-century Janam Sakhi attributed to Miharban, there is a touching account of Nanak's departure for Sultanpur. Sulakhani, his wife, wailed that her world would be devastated and begged him to take her along. Nanak promises that he will arrange for her to join him as soon as he gets employment, which is precisely what happened. Later, at Kartarpur, Sulakhani is upset with the Guru when she sees Lehina clad in a milk-white cotton outfit carrying drenched grass from the fields. She asks him: "Why do you make him carry this muddy grass?" The Guru affectionately explains: "O dearest, this sheaf of wet grass is his throne." The allusion is to Lehina's forthcoming succession. It is likely that the residents of Kartarpur were expected to follow this model of warm and affectionate family life with its respect and love for the lady of the house.

Earlier reference was made to Mata Khivi, the wife of Guru Angad, helping in the *langar* (see p. 30). Sikh tradition has also retained memory of how their daughter, Bibi Amro, was instrumental in bringing Amardas, later Guru Amardas, to the Sikh center at Khadur. There are traditions that imply that Bibi Bhani played a role in her father, Guru Amardas's, choice of his successor. The chariot which Mata Ganga, the wife of Guru Arjan, used for traveling is preserved as a precious possession of the community at Bhai Rupa, a village in southern Punjab.

Seventeenth-century documents add to the picture in interesting ways. An early manuscript containing Sikh liturgical compositions is attributed to Guru Hargobind, who arranged to have it compiled for the use of Bibi Viro, his only daughter. Another manuscript, which contains sacred writings as well as stories attributed to the Gurus, was given as a wedding present to Bibi Rupo, Guru Harirai's daughter. Its text has an intriguing set of entries of the death dates of the women in the Guru lineage. Guru Tegh Bahadur's naming of his town Chak Nanaki, after his mother, is also significant.

Two letters of command written by Mata Gujari, the wife of Guru Tegh Bahadur, asking congregations in the east to send some goods to Anandpur have survived. This tradition continued when the wives of Guru Gobind Singh, Mata Sundari and Mata Sahib Devi wrote to different congregations, reminding them of their responsibility toward the Guru's family. Mata Jito's presence at the original administering of the *khande di pahul* (see p. 40) cannot be overstated. Mata Bassi, one of the daughters-in-law of Guru Hargobind, played an important role in family matters, including overseeing the succession ceremony of her younger brother-in-law, Guru Tegh Bahadur. Punjab Kaur provided leadership to one of the Sikh dissident groups after her husband Ramrai's death in Dehradun in 1687.

All these examples underscore the fact that women in the Gurus' families participated fully in Sikh life. They had access to learning and were encouraged to read sacred literature. They played an important role in their immediate families and represented their husbands if the need arose. They enjoyed respect in the community to the degree that a town could be named after them, and their death dates were significant enough to be recorded in a scriptural manuscript. Though evidence is limited, the model may well be true of Sikh society at large. Bebe Peri Bai, a leader in the congregation at Patna, is consistently mentioned in Guru Tegh Bahadur's letters, and Mai Bhago is believed to have led forty Sikhs back into the battle after their initial parting of ways with Guru Gobind Singh. It is quite likely that there were other important female figures in the Sikh community whose lives and deeds were not recorded.

In the post-Guru period, Bibi Pradhan Kaur (d. 1789), daughter of Baba Ala Singh, the founder of the Patiala dynasty, is known for her spirituality and for the school for children she started at Barnala, which was open until recently. Sada Kaur emerged as a key figure and played a significant role in placing Ranjit Singh, her son-in-law, in a position of power. Rani Jindan, the wife of Ranjit Singh, played an important role in organizing resistance to the British after the annexation of the Punjab.

Harnam Kaur worked as a teacher in the first boarding school for girls, which opened in 1894. She died at the age of twenty-four, yet her accomplishment there seems to have been so impressive that she became the subject of a biography, published in 1908. From this point on, Sikh women could be seen excelling in all spheres of life. For instance, there are Simi Garewal (acting), Inderjit Kaur Sandhu (education), Gurinder Chadha (films), Daljit Dhaliwal (journalism), Amrita Pritam and Dalip Kaur Tiwana (literature), Amrita Shergill, Phoolan Rani (painting), Rajinder Kaur Bhattal, Jagir Kaur (politics), Surinder Kaur (singing), Neelam Man Singh (theater), to name just a few. Sikh women now outnumber their male counterparts on the university campuses of the Punjab, and they contribute considerably to the workforce in the areas of education and health. They can be seen driving, often alone, in cars and on scooters all over the Punjab, a reflection of the progress they have made.

However, not everyone agrees with this interpretation: some would like to present Guru Nanak's view of gender equality in all its strength and play down Sikh practices; others would focus on the practices and point out that Guru Nanak's nine successors, the first five Sikhs who undertook the *khaṇḍe di pahul*, and the primary leadership in later times have all been males. The discussion is even more complicated when the facts that four of the Gurus had more than one wife—Ranjit Singh had many—and that female infanticide has not been entirely alien to Sikh society are considered. A 2001 census in the Punjab recorded a male to female ratio of 1,000 males to 874 females. The question must be asked then: have the Sikhs as a society failed to translate their gender-related beliefs of equality into actual practice?

It is true that Guru Nanak's ideas evolved within the parameters of the institution of patriarchy. His support for women emerged from his emphasis on the family as the basic unit of a community as well as from his support for the oppressed. This approach is more akin to a humanist's rather than a feminist's point of view, and augmented the tradition's positive attitude toward the presence of women in the community, while maintaining an overall framework of patriarchy. All the women from the Kartarpur period remain in Guru Nanak's shadow, but that they emerge at all may be an achievement when compared with complete silence around female members of other spiritual leaders, such as Kabir and Ravidas.

The little information there is also comes into focus when placed against the backdrop of Punjabi culture, which continues to sing of the father roaring on the housetop if the newborn baby is a boy and bemoaning his lot if it is a daughter. Guru Nanak created a setting in which a plethora of positive opportunities was offered to women as equal members of the community. At a wedding ceremony in 1977, in Mandi Dabwali, a sleepy town in southern Punjab, the bride's friends announced that she would lead the groom in the final circumambulation around the Guru Granth. Sikh savants sitting in the congregation found the decision puzzling, but could not offer any doctrinal objection to it. In the late 1990s, some Sikh women of European and American origins sought permission from the SGPC to perform ritual washing of the inner part of the Darbar Sahib at midnight, an historically male practice. The men who had done the service earlier were uncomfortable but the SGPC authorities granted permission. Changing such entrenched traditions takes time, patience, and leadership, but Sikh women have firm doctrinal support to claim their equal rights if they decide to do so.

At the turn of the twenty-first century

The present-day world Sikh community encompasses three groups: the Sikhs who are living in the Punjab (17 million); the Sikhs who live in other parts of India (4 million); and the Sikhs who have moved abroad (2 million). In the Punjab, the Sikhs constitute 67 per cent of the total population, and this regional majority puts them in a far more comfortable situation than, say, the Christians, the Jains, and the Muslims, which are prominent religious minorities in India. The SGPC and the Akali Dal serve as custodians of Sikh religious and political interests, respectively. Developments in the agricultural sector in the 1960s boosted the Punjab's economy, and, though the dividends have tapered off in recent decades (see p. 111), the state continues to be more prosperous than other parts of the subcontinent.

Sikh religious life continues to evolve and thrive. In 1966, as already mentioned, the Sikhs formally recognized the status of the Damdama Sahib, Talvandi Sabo, as that of a Takhat, raising it to become one of the five sacred centers under the Darbar Sahib, Amritsar. In the 1990s, they created a sophisticated facility at Goindval to cremate the old texts of the Guru Granth, which replaced the earlier tradition of disposing of them in flowing water (*jal parvah*). If the introduction of print media initiated the generation of the codified statements of Rahit a century ago, the present-day televising of the morning and evening ceremonies at the Darbar Sahib is bringing a new level of standardization to Sikh ceremonial activity: now all gurdwaras tend to follow precisely the same daily routine as the Darbar Sahib.

Like other communities, the Sikhs have their zones of tension. On the religious level, Sikh leadership is acutely aware of areas where Sikh practice falls short of the ideal. While Sikh beliefs recognize the authority of the Guru Granth and the Guru Panth, which leaves no space for personal authority in religious matters, the Punjabi landscape is studded with the seats of numerous Sikh saints, who enjoy the authority of modifying the religious practice of their followers. Since the eighteenth century, the Rahit literature has made repeated injunctions against visiting the sites of popular deities and patron saints, but many Sikhs continue to participate in the vernacular culture, in addition to visiting Hindu temples and Muslim sites. Finally, the goal of removing social and gender differences within Sikh society has made only a limited headway. Women may play a full role in devotional life, yet positions of leadership remain in male hands. Marriages between different social groups are still uncommon.

In the political sphere, the Sikhs find themselves in a complicated situation. Having failed to create a separate Sikh state in 1947, the Akali Dal leadership has struggled to reshape its vision of sovereignty to fit into the setup of a modern state. In the 1950s,

IN FOCUS

Sikh art

SIKH CULTURAL HERITAGE includes architecture, art, literature, music, and numismatics. Painting is the oldest art form and Sikh art originated in the illuminated manuscripts of sacred texts, the earliest example of which is contained in the Goindval Pothis (1570s). The Goindval Pothis were inscribed in stylized Gurmukhi calligraphy with the opening folios illuminated in blue and gold. Later, the tradition of Gurmukhi calligraphy continued (see the title page) and the illumination work in some cases extended to encompass the entire text of the Guru Granth.

The manuscripts of the Janam Sakhis provided another arena for artistic expression. From 1658, the extant manuscripts contain miniatures that illustrate episodes from Guru Nanak's life. He is shown sitting among his family members (see p. 19), debating with fellow religious leaders, and meeting ordinary people. He is portrayed in natural settings among trees, birds, animals, lush green vegetation, and occasionally with a cityscape in the background. These illustrations were transposed to Sikh murals in the late seventeenth century.

This period also witnessed the creation of individual portraits of the Gurus, and there is a contemporary portrait of Guru Gobind Singh as a royal figure with an attendant waving a peacock flywhisk (see p. 43). A manuscript of the Guru Granth created in 1723 contains the miniature portraits of both Guru Nanak and Guru Gobind Singh pasted on its opening folios. These portraits later appeared on some Sikh coins, and pictures of the other Gurus also began to be popularized.

Beginning in the late eighteenth century, the rise in Sikh political power attracted scribes (*katib*), artists (*musavar*), and mural painters (*naqash*) from the hills and Rajasthan, resulting in the flourishing of Sikh-sponsored art. Bhai Gurdas and Bhai Mani Singh, two Sikh scholars, entered Sikh iconography, and simultaneously, Sikh nobility became a significant subject of artistic rendering. The murals at the Darbar Sahib used floral and animal motifs and brought to a peak the earlier tradition of illumination of scriptural manuscripts.

Portrait of painter's wife. S.G. Thakur Singh. Oil on canvas, 1960.

The murals of the Akal Takhat followed the Janam Sakhi tradition of illustrated stories from the lives of the Gurus.

The arrival of European painters at the Sikh court in the mid-nineteenth century introduced Sikh artists to three-dimensional perspective, painting in oil, the use of canvas, and the selection of subjects from everyday life. The establishment of the Mayo School of Art in Lahore in 1875, and the arrival of photography and the printing press in the region, transformed the existing artistic forms into large-scale production.

S.G. Thakur Singh (1899–1976), the leading Sikh painter of the twentieth century (see page 108), started his career by winning the runner-up painting award for "After Bath," in the London exhibition of Commonwealth Art in 1924. He went on to pioneer a school of art in Amritsar, in which painters trained at the Mayo School and schools in London worked. From among this group, Hari Singh (1894–1970), Gurdit Singh (1901–81) and Kirpal Singh (1923–90) played an important role in the building of the Central Sikh Museum at the Darbar Sahib. Sobha Singh (1901–1986) made a name for himself as a calendar artist portraying the Gurus. At present, Jarnail Singh (b. 1956) and R.M. Singh (b. 1965) continue this tradition of figurative painting, while many other Sikh painters have turned to abstract art.

The Amritsar school of painters made portraits of the Gurus, depicted scenes from Sikh history, created architectural paintings of the Darbar Sahib from different angles and at different times of the day, and drew scenes from Punjabi life. In the portrayal of Sikh history and culture, they used a style characterized by realistic depictions of daily life, often using real people as models.

The movement of Sikhs away from the Punjab has had an interesting effect on Sikh art. Jarnail Singh moved to Vancouver, Canada, in the late 1990s but has continued his work on earlier themes, unaffected by the change in culture and scenery. At present, he is involved in creating murals from Sikh history in a gurdwara building in Surrey, Vancouver. Shivdev Singh, a physician who left medicine and underwent training in art in the United States, on the other hand, has been painting Californian and European landscapes since 1990. The Singh twins, Amrit and Rabindra, Sikh painters who were born in London, England, draw on the Indian miniature tradition to "explore cultural, social, and political issues of global significance."

The twentieth century also witnessed an interest in the preservation of Sikh artistic heritage. M.S. Randhawa (1909–86), an art connoisseur, was instrumental in creating museums at Amritsar, Anandpur, Chandigarh, and Ludhiana. More recently, the collection and preservation of Sikh art outside India has begun to preoccupy Sikhs living abroad. Narinder Singh Kapany, a leading collector of Sikh art in the United States, has made a significant contribution in this direction. In the past few years, he has successfully involved the Victoria and Albert Museum, London, and the Museum of Asian Art, San Francisco, in the exhibition of Sikh art. Forrest McGill has recently organized "The Sikh Kingdoms," a permanent exhibit at the Museum of Asian Art, and Paul Taylor is working toward creating a Sikh gallery in their "Hall of Asian Cultures" at the Smithsonian Museum, Washington D.C. Sikh artistic heritage is thus represented in two major art centers in the United States.

they participated in state government by aligning with the Congress. The ideological differences between the two were further compounded by personal rivalries between the Akali Dal and the Congress Sikh leaders. The experiment failed, and the potential of this collaboration has never been tested again.

The Akali Dal's demand for a linguistic state within the Indian constitutional boundaries was another version of the same effort. Once the Punjabi-speaking state came into being, the Akali Dal leadership created an opposition front, which included political parties ranging from the Hindu nationalists to the Communists. Under the leadership of Prakash Singh Badal, however, this model became restricted to collaboration between the Akali Dal and the Hindu nationalist Bharatiya Janata Party (BJP), currently the ruling party in New Delhi.

The Akali Dal–BJP alignment has provided Badal with political security but there are serious problems inherent in it. On the ideological level, the Akali Dal leadership sees itself as the custodian of the political interests of the Sikh community, and believes it possesses a distinct culture, history, language, and territory. For the BJP ideologues, Indians are divided into two religious groups: the Muslims and Christians, a group which is considered to be the legacy of foreign invaders, and all others, seen as part of the larger Hindu fold. Furthermore, the Akali Dal stands for the interests of rural Sikhs, while the BJP represents the urban traders. The clash between these conflicting agendas does not bode well for the long-term relationship.

Although efforts are being made to adjust Sikh political aspirations to contemporary realities, the idea of Sikh sovereignty continues to have a strong pull. Sant Bhindranwale received ample support when he raised the issue of independence from India (see p. 68). He offered his life for this vision of sovereignty, and his sacrifice has not been forgotten. In mid-2002, the situation which brought India and Pakistan to the brink of nuclear war included, among many issues, the extradition of five Sikh leaders based in Pakistan who are alleged to have been working toward the formation of Khalistan. Simranjit Singh Mann, a Sikh member of parliament, has continued to identify with the demand for "a sovereign Sikh state to be achieved through democratic and peaceful means." His is not a solitary voice—others support this point of view, although they may be unwilling to say so in public.

A new problem has emerged recently. The Sikhs have historically been attached to the Punjabi landscape. In recent decades, however, agricultural methods have undergone fundamental changes. Intensive farming, using excessive irrigation, fertilizers, and pesticides, has taken its toll, depleting the water table, damaging the soil, and adversely affecting the environment. The land that the Sikhs believed to have come to them as a gift from the Gurus and Vahiguru may be heading toward an environmental disaster. It is only recently that discussions about reclaiming the soil and the diversification of the crops have been initiated. On festival days at the Kesgar Sahib, Anandpur, authorities distribute blessings (*prashad*) in the form of tree saplings for pilgrims to take home.

Finding long-term solutions to these challenges may not be easy, and contemporary Punjabi Sikh leadership has shown little willingness to address them. Since Operation Bluestar in 1984 (see p. 69), no serious ideological reflection on the long-term goals of the community has taken place. The concerns of Sikh leadership have been primarily restricted to personal squabbles. As a result, future directions have not yet been charted. While the dream of Sikh sovereignty remains part of the Sikhs' symbolic landscape, it is yet to be seriously debated as to which of the options—standing by itself, continued alignment with BJP, or working with the Congress—would be most beneficial for the Akali Dal.

The movement of Sikh traders to other parts of India dates back to the sixteenth century, since when they have created small communities in urban centers such as Agra, Bidar, Burhanpur, Banaras, Delhi, Patna and so on. In the twentieth century, Sikh farmers bought lands in the present-day western Uttar Pradesh, Haryana, and Rajasthan and settled there. At present three million Sikhs live in these three states and Delhi, and the remaining one million are spread all over the country. By and large, they have done well in their new homes.

The Sikh relationship with the overwhelming Hindu majority is, however, complicated. Sikhs have to deal with Hindu leadership's fundamental belief that the Sikhs are part of the Hindu religious fold, on the one hand, and they have to be ready to resist the backlash against the rise of Sikh separatism in the Punjab, on the other. This helplessness became evident following Mrs. Gandhi 's assassination. In places such as Delhi, Hindu mobs avenged her death by lynching several thousand Sikhs. The primary energy of the Sikhs in other parts of India, particularly those living in urban settings, will have thus to be invested in keeping their religious identity intact and in surviving.

Finally, the Sikhs who live away from the Indian subcontinent have moved into an unprecedented situation with significant implications for the future of the Sikh community. The simple fact that they live in alien cultures is having an impact on Sikh life in a wide variety of ways. The essential ceremonies remain unchanged but they are couched in a new reality. For instance, the bones of the deceased continue to be taken to Kiratpur by many Sikh families, as is done in the Punjab, but the rituals associated with public mourning and the placement of the dead body on the pyre are modified to conform to the setting of the funeral homes.

Changes have occurred to important Sikh institutions such as the *langar*. In many gurdwaras, the *langar* is organized along the lines of a buffet meal, where one helps oneself to food, takes it to a table, and eats it there. The spirit of the *langar* centered on charity and service is preserved, but the outer forms of *langar* have changed. In Western countries, old church buildings have been bought and modified to serve as gurdwaras, thus bringing interesting architectural changes to the layout of sacred space.

This is the first time in Sikh history that the intertwining of Sikh beliefs and Punjabi cultural practices is in the process of becoming analyzed and separated, and the resulting evolution is extended to fundamental beliefs such as the Sikh relationship with the land of the Punjab. Slowly but surely, a new distinction is emerging in Sikh diasporic thinking. The Punjab is seen as the sacred land. From Australia to North America, Sikhs hold various citizenships yet are united under this concept of holy land.

Language-related issues are the most complicated ones. Since the founding of the community in the sixteenth century, Sikhs have manifested an intense pride in the fact that their literature is written in Punjabi and in the Gurmukhi script; these vessels of communication are close to the core of their sense of identity. Hence historically there has been little wavering from a doctrinal insistence on the importance of understanding the sacred Sikh writings in their original form. These are not verses to be merely chanted, but to be understood, and their message must be observed in the daily lives of all Sikhs. With increasing numbers of Sikhs born outside the Punjab, however, the traditional insistence that religion needs to proceed in the vernacular—the common regional language and life—has radically new implications. As more and more Sikh children grow up away from the Punjab, Sikhs are beginning to accept the Guru Granth transliterated in Roman script or even in English translation, in place of (or in addition to) the original version.

While this slow process of change has been taking its course, the past three decades have seen an increase in conscious reflection and debate on the issues confronting the Sikh community around the world. These debates have been far livelier in countries such as Britain, Canada, and the United States. There is a consensus that Sikhs need to educate mainstream society about their unique identity, which involves telling them about Sikh heritage, Sikh beliefs, and the significance of Sikh symbols. (See page 113.) This is particularly important for Sikh children born and brought up in foreign countries and for those who are married to non-Sikhs and need to explain the intricacies of their beliefs to their spouses and children.

Sikh scholars teaching in universities in the Punjab have been invited to lecture at gurdwaras. This trend continues even while the focus has shifted to local scholars and universities. Mark Juergensmeyer, a sociologist of religion who had spent time in the Punjab in the 1960s, was the first to respond. With financial help coming largely from the National Endowment for the Humanities, he organized an international conference at the University of California, Berkeley, in 1976. At this event, Juergensmeyer issued a clarion call, asking his fellow comparative religionists to weave the study of Sikhism into their work, and was instrumental in opening the doors for community–university collaboration.

This initiative bore fruit in a series of Sikh studies programs at various Canadian and American universities, including the University of Toronto (1986–92), the University of British Columbia (1987–97), Columbia University (1989–99), the University of Michigan (1989–), the University of California at Santa Barbara (1999–), and Hofstra University, New York (2001–). Moreover, the teaching, publications, and conferences held under the auspices of these programs have raised the debate on Sikh heritage to a new level of sophistication. W.H. McLeod, a New Zealander, who worked in the Punjab in the mid-1960s, emerged as the central figure in Sikh studies in the West. There is now a whole new generation of scholars, which includes both Sikhs and non-Sikhs, who are writing on Sikh issues. If there is need for an expert's opinion on issues pertaining to Sikh beliefs, it is not hard to locate someone to help.

In addition to helping develop an academic understanding of the tradition, the Sikhs in these countries have become interested in saving the Sikh religious and artistic heritage. Overseas-based organizations have spread their wings to India and Pakistan. Under the stewardship of Bhai Mohinder Singh, the British Birmingham-based Guru Nanak Nishkam Sevak Jatha restored the structures of the Darbar Sahib's domes, and the buildings at Anandpur and Nander. The Association of Sikh Professionals (ASP) based in the United States has distributed well over $3.5 million dollars to various Sikh philanthropic projects in the past two decades. A California-based group is now planning to establish a treatment plant for the purification of the water in the Darbar Sahib pool.

Vaisakhi celebration at the Lincoln Memorial, Washington D.C., April 1999. Photograph. *

This level of activity indicates that Sikh societies in Britain and North America are in a considerably higher degree of animation than in any other part of the world, including the Punjab. The new environments in which Sikhs now live have provided them with fertile ground to practice their religious beliefs while separated from Punjabi cultural norms. Indeed, creating a Sikh society without social and gender distinctions may now be made possible in these dispersed communities. Scholars trained in the West are also examining the Sikh tradition from a feminist perspective, and a post-modernist perspective, while others, including this author, are continuing with traditional modes of inquiry. This multidisciplinary research, as it reaches fruition, will present a comprehensive understanding of the Sikh tradition and may pave the way for next re-formation of the Sikh tradition.

Glossary

Adi Granth (*ādi granth*) "original book": Sikh scripture contains compositions of six Sikh Gurus, a group of bards from within the Sikh community, and selections from the writings of fifteen saints of Hindu and Sufi backgrounds. The Guru Granth is the honorific title used for the text.

Akal Takhat (*akāl takhat*) "Throne of the Timeless": historically came into being as seat of the temporal authority of Guru Hargobind, and later developed into the central place from where communal decisions are announced. It is located on the premises of the Darbar Sahib.

Akali (*akālī*) "devotee of Akal/Vahiguru": the title designates Sikh warriors; also signifies member of the Akali Dal.

Akali Dal (*akālī dal*) "army of the Akalis": the political party of the Sikhs, which came into being in the early twentieth century.

akhaṇḍ paṭh (*akhaṇḍ pāṭh*) "unbroken reading": an uninterrupted recitation of the entire text of the Guru Granth by a group of readers.

Amritdhari (*amritdhārī*) "the bearer of the nectar": Sikhs who have undergone the ceremony of *khaṇḍe di pahul*, and follow the Rahit in its entirety.

ardas (*ardās*) "petition": the prayer at the closing of congregational worship.

Baba (*bābā*) "father/grandfather": a term of affection and respect often used for religious figures, including the Guru Granth.

Bhai (*bhāī*) "brother": a title applied to Sikhs of acknowledged learning and piety, or any Sikh congregational leader.

charan pahul (*charan pahul*) "nectar of the feet": the initiation ceremony in early Sikh community.

Darbar Sahib (*darbār sāhib*) "honorable court": originally built in the 1580s, the site now serves as the center of Sikh sacred geography.

Dasam Granth (*dasam granth*) "the tenth book/the book of the tenth Guru": a text containing the compositions created at Guru Gobind Singh's court.

degh tegh fateh (*degh tegh fateh*) "cauldron, sword, victory": Sikh insignia marking the community's obligation to feed the hungry and fight for the establishment of a just regime.

dharmsala (*dharamsālā*) "place for temporary residence": in early Sikh usage, a place for congregational worship.

dharmyudh (*dharmyudh*) "war in defense of *dharm*" (duty): it implies a political struggle with religious overtones.

din-duniya (*dīn-dunīya*) "religious and temporal [concerns]": signifies close relationship between religion and politics in Sikh beliefs.

giani (*gianī*) "a learned man": a scholar well versed in Sikh scriptures.

granth (*granth*) "book": scripture.

granthi (*granthī*) "keeper of the Guru Granth": the official in charge of the gurdwara. He leads congregational worship, and performs ceremonies such as weddings and the naming of newborn children.

gurdwara (*gurdvārā / gurduārā*) "Guru's house": Sikh place of worship. The key area of a gurdwara is a spacious room housing the Guru Granth, where people sit and listen to scriptural recitation and singing. The gurdwara always has a *langar* and a Nishan Sahib.

gurmat (*gurmat*) "the advice of the Gurus": the sum total of the Gurus' teachings.

gurmata (*gurmatā*) "the intention of the Guru": the will of the eternal Guru, as expressed in a formal decision made by a representative assembly of Sikhs; a resolution of the *sarbat khalsa*.

Gurmukhi (*gurmukhī*) "the script of the Gurmukhs / Sikhs": the script of the Guru Granth.

gurpurb (*gurpurb*) "the festival of the Guru": celebration of the birth or death anniversary of one of the Gurus.

Guru (*gurū*) "preceptor": the mode of Vahiguru as teacher, which in the past was revealed to Sikhs in the ten human Gurus, and persists in the form of the Guru Granth and the Guru Panth.

Guru Granth (*gurū granth*) " the honorable Guru in book form": see Adi Granth

Guru Panth (*gurū panth*) "community as the Guru": the doctrine of the authoritative presence of the eternal Guru in a Sikh assembly.

haumai (*haumai*) "self-centeredness": the powerful impulse to disregard submission to Vahiguru and instead succumb to personal gratification.

hukam (*hukam*) "order": the command of Vahiguru; reply from the Guru Granth to supplication at the closing of worship.

hukamnama (*hukamnāmā*) "decree": letter of the Gurus; a decree announced at the Akal Takhat, considered to be binding on the entire community.

Janam-sakhi (*janam-sākhī*) "birth story": traditional narratives of Guru Nanak.

Japji (*japjī*): a composition of Guru Nanak which is recited by Sikhs every morning. This is the most commonly known Sikh prayer.

Jaṭ (*jaṭ*): from a nomadic background, the Jaṭs comprise the majority of the Sikhs.

jatha (*jathā*) "military detachment": organized group of Sikhs with a particular mission of preaching and reform or a political agenda.

Jathedar (*jathedār*) "commander": the title of a leader of a Sikh band; custodians of the five takhats (thrones).

kachha (*kachhā*) "pair of shorts." *Kachha, kes, kangha, kirpan,* and *kara* constitute the five items which an Amritdahri Sikh is required to wear.

kangha (*kanghā*) "comb." See *kachha.*

kaṛa (*kaṛā*) "steel bracelet." See *kachha.*

karah prashad (*kaṛāh prashād*) "blessed food": made of flour, sugar, and clarified butter, *kaṛah prashad* is distributed after worship.

Kaur (*kaur*) "princess": used as a name by female Sikhs, parallel to Singh for men.

kes (*kes*) "hair." See *kachha.*

Kesdhari (*kesdhārī*) "hair-bearing": the Sikhs who keep their hair uncut.

Khalistan (*khālistān*) "country of the Khalsa": the proposed name for a Sikh state independent of India.

Khalsa (*khālsā*) "pure, Vahiguru's own": synonymous with Sikh, Gursikh, the term implies a pure status for the Sikh community and reiterates its belief in the authority of the Vahiguru, the revelatory content of the Guru Granth, and the creation of the Khalsa Raj.

khaṇḍe di pahul (*khaṇḍe dī pahul*) "the nectar made with the double-edged sword": the ceremony instituted by Guru Gobind Singh at the time of the declaration of the Khalsa. Those who undergo this ceremony constitute an elect group called the Amritdharis. They are expected to dedicate themselves to Vahiguru and work toward the establishment of the Khalsa Raj.

Khatri (*khatrī*) "merchant-castes": Khatri refers to a cluster of merchant castes, such as the Bedis, Bhallas, and Sodhis.

kirpan (*kirpān*) "sword." See *kachha.*

kirtan (*kīrtan*) "devotional singing": a significant part of Sikh piety.

langar (*langar*) "community kitchen": attached to every gurdwara, food is served to all, regardless of age, creed, gender, or social distinctions.

mangal (*mangal*): the invocation appearing at the head of the text of the Guru Granth. It reads: "One Supreme Being, the Eternal Reality, the Creator, without fear or enmity, immortal, never incarnated, self-existent, known through the grace of the Guru."

manji (*manjī*): "cot": seat of authority in the early Sikh community.

Masand (*masand*) "[Guru's] deputy": authorized leader of a local congregation.

miri-piri (*mīrī-pīrī*) "temporal–spiritual": the assumption of temporal and spiritual authority on the part of the Gurus. See *din-duniya*.

mulmantar (*mūlmantar*). See *mangal*.

Namdhari (*nāmdhārī*) "the bearer of the Name": a nineteenth-century movement started by Baba Balak Singh. Its main base is near Ludhiana.

Nanak Panth (*nānak panth*) "the way of Nanak": term used for the early Sikh community.

Nath Yogi (*nāth yogī*): a member of a Shaivite sect of ascetics, which was very influential in medieval Punjab.

Nirankari (*nirankarī*) "a follower of Nirankar": a nineteenth-century movement started by Baba Dayal. At present its bases are in Chandigarh and Delhi.

Nishan Sahib (*nishān sāhib*) "honorable symbol": saffron flag with the insignia of *degh tegh fateh* (see above).

panj kakke (*panj kakke*) "five k's": the five items, each of whose names begins with letter "k," that an Amritdhari should wear. (See *kachha*.)

panj piare (*panj piāre*) "the beloved five": represent the Sikh community. This designation recalls the five men who offered their lives for the sake of the community at Guru Gobind Singh's call.

Panth (*panth*) "the path": community.

pothi (*pothī*) "volume," "book": title used for early Sikh manuscripts.

qaum (*kaum*) "a people who stand together": the Sikh usage of this term has connotations of both community and nation.

Rahit (*raihit*): Sikh belief and practice.

Rahit Maryada (*raihit maryādā*): Sikh belief and practice; also a specific text on the subject, first published under the auspices of the SGPC in 1950.

Rahitnama (*raihitnāmā*): manual of Sikh belief and practice.

raj karega khalsa (*raj karega khālsā*) "the *khalsa* shall rule": the phrase became popular in the 1710s as part of Sikh aspirations for sovereign rule and continues to be recited in Sikh prayers.

Ramgaria (*ramgaṛīa*): Sikhs of the carpenter background.

sangat (*sangat*) "congregation": congregational worship constitutes the heart of Sikh devotion.

Sahijdhari (*sahijdhārī*) "the bearers of slowness": those who have not undergone the *khande di pahul*, do not keep their hair uncut, do not use Singh/ Kaur in their names, but affirm allegiance to the Guru Granth.

sant (*sant*) "saint": a title for a Sikh holy person.

sarbat khalsa (*sarbat khālsā*) "the entire *khalsa*": an assembly of representatives of the whole Sikh community, historically gathered at the Akal Takhat, Amritsar, to resolve some crisis facing the Sikh community.

Sati Sri Akal (*sat srī akāl*) "Vahiguru is truth": the common Sikh greeting.

seva (*sevā*) "service": service is a key value in Sikh beliefs.

Sikh (*sikh*) "disciple/learner": any person who believes in Vahiguru, in the ten Gurus, in the Guru Granth, in the *khande di pahul*, and in the belief system of no other religion.

Singh (*singh*) "lion": the title used by male Sikhs.

Singh Sabha (*singh sabhā*) "the Singh Society": a late nineteenth-century movement dedicated to preparing Sikhs to face modernity.

Sufi (*sūfī*) "a Muslim mystic": as a group, Sufis had a major religious impact in medieval Punjab. From centers known as *khanqahs*, these saints taught their disciples, fed travelers, and gave medicine to the sick.

Takhat (*takhat*) "throne": one of the five seats of authority among Sikhs. These are the Akal Takhat, Amritsar, the Kesgar Sahib, Anandpur, the Damdama Sahib, Talvandi Sabo (all three in the Punjab), the Harimandir Sahib, Patna (in Bihar), and the Hazur Sahib, Nander (in Maharashtra).

Udasi (*udāsī*) "renunciants": an order of ascetics begun by Srichand, the son of Guru Nanak.

Vahiguru (*vahigurū*) "Wonderful Sovereign": the most commonly used epithet for God in the Sikh tradition.

Suggested Further Reading

General studies

W. Owen Cole, and P.S. Sambhi, *The Sikhs: Their Religious Beliefs and Practices* (Brighton: Sussex Academic Press, 1995).

J.S. Grewal, *The Sikhs of the Punjab* (Cambridge and New York: Cambridge University Press, 1990).

W.H. McLeod, *Sikhism* (New York and London: Penguin Books, 1997).

Art and architecture

F.S. Aijazuddin, *Sikh Portraits by European Artists* (London and New York: Sotheby Parke Bernet, 1979).

P.S. Arshi, *Sikh Architecture in Punjab* (New Delhi: Intellectual Publishing House, 1986).

B.N. Goswamy, *Piety and Splendour: Sikh Heritage in Art* (New Delhi: National Museum, 2000).

S. Stronge (ed.), *The Arts of the Sikh Kingdoms* (London: Victoria and Albert Museum, 1999).

Literature

Khushwant Singh (trans.), *Hymns of the Gurus* (New Delhi: Viking, 2003).

W.H. McLeod (trans.), *The B-40 Janam-Sakhi* (Amritsar: Guru Nanak Dev University, 1980).

W.H. McLeod (trans.), *Textual Sources for the Study of Sikhism* (Manchester: Manchester University Press, 1984, Chicago: The University of Chicago Press, 1984).

Nikky-Guninder Kaur Singh (trans.), *The Name of My Beloved: verses of the Sikh Gurus* (San Francisco: HarperSanFrancisco, 1995).

The complete text of the Guru Granth with English translation is accessible on the web at:http://www.srigranth.org/about.html. The search engine has the facility to locate information by page number, author, or a key word.

Politics

Paul R. Brass, *The Politics of India since Independence* (New York and Cambridge: Cambridge University Press, 1994).

Ainslie T. Embree, *Utopias in Conflict: Religious Nationalism in Modern India* (Berkeley: University of California Press, 1990).

Mark Juergensmeyer, *Terror in the Mind of God: The Global Rise of Religious Violence* (Berkeley: University of California Press, 2000).

Gurharpal Singh, *Ethnic Conflict in India: A Case-Study of Punjab* (New York: St. Martin's Press, 2000).

Sikhs outside the Punjab

N.G. Barrier and V.A. Dusenbery (eds.) *The Sikh Diaspora: Migration and the Experience beyond Punjab* (Columbia, Missouri: South Asia Books, 1989).

S.S. Dhami, *Maluka: A Novel* (Patiala: Punjabi University, 1997).

Kathleen D. Hall, *Lives in Translation: Sikh Youth as British Citizens* (Phildelphia: University of Pennsylvania Press, 2002).

Drashan Singh Tatla, *The Sikh Diaspora: The Search for Statehood* (Seattle: University of Washington Press, 1999).

New approaches

Brian K. Axel, *The Nation's Tortured Body: Violence, Representation, and the Formation of a Sikh Diaspora* (Durham Duke University Press, 2001).

Constance W. Elsberg, *Graceful Women: Gender and Identity in American Sikh Community* (Knoxville: University of Tennessee Press, 2003).

Dorris R. Jakobsh, *Relocating Gender in Sikh History: Transformation, Meaning and Identity* (New Delhi: Oxford University Press, 2003).

Cynthia K. Mahmood, *Fighting for Faith and Nation: Dialogues with Sikh Militants* (Philadelphia: University of Pennsylvania Press, 1997).

Harjot Oberoi, *The Construction of Religious Boundaries: Culture, Identity and Diversity in the Sikh Tradition* (New Delhi: Oxford University Press, 1994).

Nikky-Guninder KaurSingh, *The Feminine Principle in the Sikh Vision of the Transcendent* (New York and Cambridge: Cambridge University Press, 1993).

Documentaries

Sikhs. Produced by John Das, BBC Birmingham, England. The film traces the history of the community from its origins to the present time (1999).

Sikh Street. Channel 4 documentary on the Sikh community of Gravesend, England (2002).

Roots in the Sand. Produced by Jayasri Majumdar Hart. The film portrays the pioneer Punjabi settlers in Southern California's Imperial Valley (1998).

Useful websites

1. The Sikhism Home Page: www.sikhs.org
2. Gateway to Sikhism: www.allaboutsikhs.com
3. Sikhnet: www.sikhnet.com

Index

Page numbers in *italics* refer to picture captions.

Adi Granth 15, 73
Ajit Singh 44, 51
Akal Takhat 35, 53, 55, 69, *69*, 88, 89, 110
Akali Dahl 57–8, 65, 67, 70, 107, 113
Amardas, Guru 30, 31, 32, 33, 35, 36, 103
Amritdharis 99, 100
Amritsar 53, 55; Treaty of (1809) 51 *see also* Dabar Sahib
Amro, Bibi 104
Anandpur 39, 44, 45, 48, 53
Angad, Guru 30
ardas 16
Arjan, Guru 30, 31, 32, 33, 34, 35, 36, 37
art 108–11
Association of Sikh Professionals (ASP) 116
Aurangzeb, Emperor 44, 45
Avtar Singh Vahiria 60–1

Badal, Prakash Singh 70, 112
Bahadur Shah II 45, 56
Balak Singh 53
Balvand 26, 29, 30, 75–6
Banda Singh 48, 49, 94, 101

Bassi, Mata 104
Bebe Peri Bai 104–5
Bedi, Khem Singh 60–1, 63, 101
Bhago, Mai 105
Bhani, Bibi 104
Bharatiya Janata Party (BJP) 112, 113
Bhasaur, Teja Singh 60, 61, 63
Bhatts, the 34, 75
Bhindranwale, Sant Jarnail Singh 14, 67–70, 112
Bir Singh 95–6
birth 85–6
BJP (Bharatiya Janata Party) 112, 113
bracelet (*kara*) 44, 62
britches (*kachha*) 44, 62
British rule in the Punjab 51, 55–60
Budha, Baba 95

Central Sikh Museum 66, 110
Chak Nanaki 37, 38, 39
Chamars 95, 96, 99
Chando Rani 20
charan pahul 28
Chaupa Singh 42, 44, 53, 78, 88, 94
comb (*kangha*) 44, 61–2

Dabar Sahib 88–9, 108
Damdama Sahib 66, 107
Darbar Sahib 14, 31,

31, 35, 45–7, 53, 55, 68–9, 116
Dasam Granth 76–7
Dayal, Baba 53, 63
Dayal Singh Majithia 58–9
degh tegh fateh 48, *49*
dharmyudh (holy war) 83
Dit Singh 96
Divali, festival of 33, 46, 87

education 59, 66
Ek Oankar 73, *73*

family responsibilities 24, 82
Fateh Singh 44
fearlessness 38
five ks 62, 86
funerals 86

Gandhi, Indira 69, 113
Ganga, Mata 104
Gill, K.P.S. 70
Gobind Singh, Guru 15, 16, 38–45, *43*, 45, 48, 51–2, 64, 73, 74, 77, 83
Goindval 31, 33, 34
Goindval Pothis 26, 32, 73, 108
Golden Temple *see* Darbar Sahib
Grewal, J.S. 66
Gujari, Mata 44, 104
Gurbilas 75
Gurdas, Bhai 18, 28, 32, 36, 40, 75, 77,